The Famous JUDY BOLTON Mystery Stories

By MARGARET SUTTON

In Order of Publication

THE VANISHING SHADOW
THE HAUNTED ATTIC
THE INVISIBLE CHIMES
SEVEN STRANGE CLUES
THE GHOST PARADE
THE YELLOW PHANTOM
THE MYSTIC BALL
THE VOICE IN THE SUITCASE
THE MYSTERIOUS HALF CAT
THE RIDDLE OF THE DOUBLE RING
THE UNFINISHED HOUSE
THE MIDNIGHT VISITOR
THE NAME ON THE BRACELET
THE CLUE IN THE PATCHWORK QUILT
THE MARK ON THE MIRROR
THE SECRET OF THE BARRED WINDOW
THE RAINBOW RIDDLE
THE LIVING PORTRAIT
THE SECRET OF THE MUSICAL TREE
THE WARNING ON THE WINDOW
THE CLUE OF THE STONE LANTERN
THE SPIRIT OF FOG ISLAND
THE BLACK CAT'S CLUE
THE FORBIDDEN CHEST
THE HAUNTED ROAD
THE CLUE IN THE RUINED CASTLE
THE TRAIL OF THE GREEN DOLL
THE HAUNTED FOUNTAIN
THE CLUE OF THE BROKEN WING
THE PHANTOM FRIEND
THE DISCOVERY AT THE DRAGON'S MOUTH

IN THE EYE-LIKE ATTIC WINDOW SOMETHING WHITE
ROSE SLOWLY — STRETCHED ITS SKINNY ARMS —
The Haunted Attic

A JUDY BOLTON MYSTERY

THE HAUNTED ATTIC

BY

MARGARET SUTTON

GROSSET & DUNLAP
PUBLISHERS   NEW YORK

To Dorothy

CONTENTS

CONTENTS

CHAPTER I

IN DRY BROOK HOLLOW

"You could take a few of the pictures, Judy. You always admired them so."

As she spoke, Mrs. Smeed, grandmother of the pretty auburn-haired girl who knelt on the rug packing her suitcase, reached for her favorite painting.

"Don't, Grandma," Judy Bolton's slim hand stayed her. "I want to leave this room just as it is. The walls would look so bare without the pictures. Sometimes," she reflected as she closed the suitcase and turned the key, "I think it's the bare walls that make people think ghosts live in empty houses."

"So that's your idea of a haunted house?"

Judy turned suddenly to see her older brother standing in the doorway.

"Horace!" she exclaimed. "I thought you

were in Farringdon. How did you get here?
Did you fly?''

"I certainly did." He grinned and pointed
to the window. "Didn't see Arthur's Blue-
bird, did you? He and Lois want to take us all
for a ride."

Judy had not heard the handsome blue car
as it drove up to the Smeed farm house and
stopped before the door. Arthur Farringdon-
Pett, owner of the Bluebird, waited in the driv-
er's seat and his sister, Lois, leaned comfort-
ably against the cushions in the back. Judy
observed, with a pleased smile, that the place
next to Arthur had been reserved for her.

"What a nice surprise," she exclaimed as
she greeted them from the porch. "Only you'll
have to excuse my appearance. Mother and
Dad have gone to shop for new furniture and
left the packing to me."

"Just what I expected," laughed Arthur.
"Horace thought you might need him to help
so Lois and I hopped into the car and brought
him along. Mr. Lee very kindly let him off for
the afternoon."

"How nice of him!" exclaimed Judy, smiling

at her brother who stood beside her on the porch. He was beginning to look more and more like the "big newspaper man" his grandmother had prophesied that he would be. Not physically big, of course, for Horace had always been slim. As a child he had been frail and, consequently, spoiled, especially by his grandmother Smeed.

"There really isn't anything you can do to help," Judy went on. "Moving is hardly any work at all when you are just moving yourselves, the way we are. The trunks and suitcases are all packed and Dad and Mother are planning to have the furniture sent up from the stores as soon as the house is ready. All we have to take is our clothes and a few things we had stored up here at Grandma's."

"We're not taking any of her furniture?"

"No, not even a picture," Judy replied. "I guess Grandma would have given us half of her things if we had let her. She even wanted to give me the bed and dresser out of my room. Of course, I wouldn't take it. I want to keep that room just as it always was because we will still be coming here for our vacations."

"Of course," Lois agreed. "Judy, aren't you thrilled to be moving into such a mysterious house?"

"More than thrilled, Lois. Positively on pins and needles! You remember how we planned a Ghost party as soon as we find out what it is that makes people think the house is haunted. Halloween would be a good time to have it, don't you think?"

"Splendid!" Arthur agreed as he helped Judy into the car. "That will give you almost two months to investigate. Of course you can't make any definite plans until the ghosts have been explained."

"They soon will be," said Horace with a confident grin. "I am to be on the investigating committee, am I not?"

"You and your sister are the committee, as far as I can see," Arthur replied. His car was gliding along the smooth white road that curved itself down Dry Brook Hollow. "But how is said committee to begin this investigation? Such things must be done systematically, you know."

"By exploring the house systematically, from

cellar to attic," stated Horace in a matter-of-fact tone.

Judy, watching him from the front seat, could not help smiling at his mock seriousness.

"There isn't much of an attic," put in Lois. "I asked Kay Vincent, daughter of the former owner, and she told me all about the house. There's only a small entrance through the ceiling of one of the rooms upstairs."

"That kind of an attic is the most interesting of all!" cried Judy. "Are there any windows in it?"

"Just holes in the gable ends," explained Arthur. "Round holes, like eyes, and the house is painted dark red and trimmed with black. It's a spooky looking place, but your family can soon cheer it up. A coat of light paint would work wonders on it."

"We wouldn't want to paint it," Horace declared.

"Of course not," agreed his sister. "What's the use of living in a haunted house if it doesn't look haunted?"

Judy was looking forward to the whole adventure with eager anticipation. She was not

going to be frightened, of that she felt sure.
Her summer in Dry Brook Hollow had taught
her to face bigger things than imaginary
ghosts.

They had covered the three miles of white
highway and were nearing the devastated town
of Roulsville. Arthur stopped his car and
leaned forward to point out the three great
pieces of fallen concrete that used to be the
dam. Judy remembered a day when she had
watched them with terror in her heart, believ-
ing her whole family had been killed in the
flood. Her brother, Horace, remembered
watching them, too, seeing them as they split
apart and spilled the contents of that massive
concrete dam upon the helpless town, but not
upon the people. For Horace, terror-stricken
when he saw the storm coming, had raced
through Roulsville on the back of his grand-
father's colt, and warned the people before the
dam actually broke. When the flood came they
were huddled together in the park high on the
hillside, safe and sound.

Then had begun publicity and praise for
Horace and offers of money, positions and al-
most anything a boy could ask. All of these

offers he had conscientiously refused. That is, all except Harry Vincent's offer of a house in the city of Farringdon, and Judy took responsibility for that.

She had done it to help her father. Their home and all their belongings had been swept away in the flood and Dr. Bolton faced the gloomy prospect of beginning all over again. Having a house given to them was certainly a help.

At first Horace had objected but when he learned that the house was supposed to be haunted and that no one else would live in it, he had forgiven his sister's boldness. The idea of solving such a mystery fascinated brother and sister alike.

Suddenly Lois surprised them by remarking, "There is a ghost in that house, really. Donald Carter says he heard it talk."

"Heard the ghost talk?" questioned Judy breathlessly.

"He says he would swear to it," she replied. "It was about a month ago when the last family moved out. Donald and some other boys were there and he solemnly declared that he had heard something call out to them in a voice that sounded spooky enough to be a 'Whopper of a Ghost.'"

Horace laughed, telling Lois that Donald Carter, being another newspaper reporter like himself, was good at making up stories.

"I wish it were more than a made up story," sighed Judy. "Plenty of people think the house is haunted and even if it isn't, it looks spooky, and that's something."

"You bet!" cried Horace. "We'll bring the ghosts out in the air if it's in our power."

CHAPTER II

ALL the way home they talked over their plans for solving the haunted house mystery. Judy felt sure that all of the strange happenings would be explained by Halloween.

"Even the voice, Lois. And the best part of it is that you and Arthur will be at the party. And Lorraine," she added as an afterthought.

"I wouldn't worry about Lorraine Lee, if I were you," Arthur advised her. "She's determined not to be friendly."

"And I'm determined to make a friend of her," Judy declared. "You just wait and see. I believe I can."

Horace agreed. He had great faith, and not without reason, in his sister's ability to do whatever he set out to do. But Arthur looked dubious.

"Lorraine is a peculiar girl, Judy. She never makes a new friend without some good reason. If Mrs. Lee had not been my mother's

9

chum I doubt if Lorraine would be friendly
with us now.''

''I think she would,'' Lois replied and her
dark eyes narrowed. ''Lorraine likes us for
our social position. She thinks that's all there
is to being nice.''

Had they quarreled, Judy wondered. Every-
one knew that Lois and Lorraine were in-
separable. People spoke of them much as one
speaks of a cup and saucer or a needle and
thread. Lois' dark eyes and hair contrasted
with Lorraine's blonde beauty, making each
girl more attractive when in company with the
other. But lately Lois had preferred Judy's
company to Lorraine's.

Arthur had brought the car to a stop in front
of the Smeed farm house and Judy's grand-
mother had invited him and his sister to stay
for dinner. Mrs. Smeed thought it was quite
a privilege to entertain Arthur who was tall
and distinguished looking. His family were
the Farringdons for whom the city of Farring-
don was named.

Judy also felt that knowing the Farringdon-
Petts was a decided asset. She fully expected
to be popular at high school. She was very

fond of Lois and felt sure she would be equally fond of her friends. Lorraine Lee, the only one whom she had met, was a vision of loveliness. Lorraine's father was the editor of the Farringdon *Daily Herald* and Judy's brother, Horace, one of the reporters. Lorraine, however, was as proud as she was beautiful. Arthur was right, it might be hard to win her friendship but Judy thought it was well worth trying. Her Halloween party ought to help.

After dinner, when Lois suggested a stroll, Judy could not conceal her pleasure.

"Suppose we go down in the beech grove," she suggested. "That knoll beside Dry Brook is my favorite nook."

"Wonderful!" exclaimed Lois. "I have a surprise for you but it had to wait until we could be alone."

There had been a frost and the green of Dry Brook Hollow had changed to flaming red and yellow. Patches of blue sky peeped through gay-colored foliage and leafy shadows danced in the sunshine. The girls walked on in silence, drinking deep of the beauty that surrounded them.

"I could write a poem about it," said Judy

at last, "but words couldn't quite say it all, could they?"

"No," answered her friend, "we just have to feel it. I hoped it would be this way."

They seated themselves on a grassy knoll under a beech tree. A shower of beech nut burrs greeted them as a playful breeze scattered treasures for industrious squirrels.

Suddenly Lois said, "Judy, let me take your hand."

Wondering, she held it out while Lois slipped a ruby ring on her finger.

"Oh!" gasped Judy. "Isn't it beautiful! But I ought not to take it, really. It wouldn't be right."

"It wouldn't be right not to take it," declared Lois, "after I bought it for you. You see, this ring isn't just an ordinary gift. It's a friendship ring because I am always going to be your friend and you are always going to be mine. Whenever you look at that ring you must think of me."

"How wonderful! But Lois, I ought to give you something in return—so that you will think of me too."

"That's all right," explained Lois. "I have

this ring Lorraine Lee gave me. That's a friendship ring too and it is very precious."

"Did you give Lorraine one too and was it —was it—like this?"

"Yes, the ring was just like this and my friendship for Lorraine means a great deal. But Lorraine's ring was stolen when some one broke into their house last summer. I wanted to get her another but she still hopes the robbers will be caught and her own ring returned."

"Oh! I hope they are. It would be terrible to lose a friendship ring. Lois, did the robbers take anything else?"

"Oh, of course. You didn't think they would break into a house just for the sake of taking one little ruby ring?"

"No, not if they were professional burglars," Judy admitted. "Tell me, what else did they take?"

Lois thought a minute. "There were so many things, Mrs. Lee's pearls and a bracelet with small diamonds in it. There were other rings taken too and some of Mr. Lee's lodge pins, cuff links and, oh, I don't know what all. Anyway they offered five hundred dollars for the recovery of all the jewels."

"They must have been valuable!" exclaimed Judy and then she was silent. "What an opportunity!" she thought to herself. Here was a chance to win Lorraine's friendship in the way she enjoyed most. But how to go about recovering lost jewels without a single clue was quite another matter.

"Judy, you're so quiet," observed Lois.

The doctor's daughter looked up with a start. "I didn't mean to be rude. I—I really ought to give you something in exchange for the ring." Judy fingered the necklace that she wore about her neck, small blue beads fastened together with a slender gold chain. "Would these be all right?" she asked. "I wore them at the spelling bee when I won the prize."

"But Horace gave them to you. Would he like it?"

Judy explained that she was sure her brother would understand her reason for giving them away. "It wouldn't be a friendship pact," she finished, "unless I gave you something precious."

Lois took them reluctantly. Then, with a pen knife, the two girls carved their initials on the tree and walked home arm in arm.

It did not occur to Judy that the friendship pact with Lois might be her greatest obstacle in winning the affection of Lois' beautiful, golden-haired friend.

Arthur was all ready to leave and he started Bluebird's motor humming as soon as the girls came in sight.

"We'll see you in Farringdon," he called out as Lois climbed into the car beside him.

"And you, Judy," Lois reminded her, "don't forget to call for me Monday on the way to school. We'll both be in Girls' High."

"And Lorraine too?"

"Yes, and Kay Vincent and Connie Gray and Marge and Betty—" She stopped speaking suddenly and caught Judy's hand.

"I meant to ask you something and almost forgot. Judy, don't tell any of the girls who gave you that ring—not any of Lorraine's crowd."

"You want me to promise that?"

"Yes, on your honor."

"All right, Lois. On my honor," Judy answered quickly without taking time to consider how difficult it might be to keep such a promise.

CHAPTER III

"WELL," began Horace, as soon as Arthur's car was out of sight around the bend in the road, "I suppose we might do some more packing before it gets dark."

"Yes," agreed Judy, "Dad will expect us to be all ready when he and Mother come home. I suppose we will start early in the morning. Seems funny, doesn't it, to be moving with nothing but trunks and suitcases?"

"There will be a crate too," Horace reminded her. "You're not leaving Blackberry behind?"

"Indeed not!" Judy caught up the black ball of a kitten and gave him an affectionate hug. He had been named Blackberry because he looked just like a round, luscious berry dipped in sugar. He was all black but his feet and the tip of his nose.

The crate was made ready but Blackberry was not confined to it until the next day when they were ready to start. Dr. Bolton decided to make two trips. First he would take Horace, Judy, Blackberry and a couple of suitcases; also two brooms and a mop. Then he would come back and get Mrs. Bolton and the trunks.

"We're going to set you to work right away," he laughed. "I haven't seen the house yet but I talked with Mr. Vincent and he seems to think it will need cleaning."

"Did you get the furniture?" questioned Judy. The idea of having all new furniture pleased her.

"All but your room," he replied, his eyes twinkling. "I had an idea you would like to choose that yourself."

"You dear!" she exclaimed, hugging him. Then her face sobered. "Don't let me spend too much, Dad. I want your office and your waiting room to be just as nice as they were in Roulsville."

"You help me arrange them," he teased her, "and they will be."

Dr. Bolton's car, a serviceable if not a luxurious one, was piled with suitcases and brooms. Horace playfully flourished one aloft as he waved goodbye to his mother and grandmother waiting on the porch. Grandfather Smeed called his goodbye from the fields where he was working with the team.

All at once Judy felt a sudden tightening at her throat, as if she wanted to cry.

"We're leaving it all behind," she said.

"We'll come back to Dry Brook Hollow to visit," Horace told her.

But both of them knew that they would never come back to the devastated Roulsville and their old home that had been washed away.

Most of the road to Farringdon went through sparsely populated farm land. Before long Judy became interested in scenery and forgot to be homesick. The road was new, only completed that summer, and the car rolled along as smoothly as had Arthur's more expensive one.

Gradually town houses began to appear and soon, with a jolt, the car came onto brick pavement and the ride through Farringdon began.

The city was, as Judy had imagined it, a beautiful place. Main Street was lined with fashionable shops displaying all the latest styles. Where Grove and Main Streets met, the public square, a park with monuments, benches and trees, gave a spaciousness to the busy section. The court house, a gray stone building with a steeple and a clock, stood in the center of the public square.

As Dr. Bolton turned the car up Grove Street, no more shops and office buildings were to be seen. In their place were wide lawns, tall shade trees and luxurious homes with colonial doors and brass knockers.

Judy had forgotten everything else as she watched. Such splendor, seen for the first time, held her spellbound. Scenery had been beautiful in Dry Brook Hollow, but farm houses and outbuildings had spoiled it. In Roulsville the houses had been neat but small and all of them nearly alike. There had been no very rich and no very poor people in Roulsville.

Here, however, every tree and shrub looked as if it had been placed on purpose to lend enchantment to the dwellings.

"Lois lives somewhere along here," remarked Horace.

"I knew she would," Judy answered quietly. "She told me about it. Oh, Horace, is that it, behind those trees?"

All that could be seen of the "house with turrets" from the street was the stone gate that marked the entrance and three towers that just peeped over the top of a pine grove and a tall barberry hedge brilliant with berries. Nothing of the lake with swans or the fountain but Lois had said they were there and how many other undiscovered wonders there were Judy dared not guess.

"And tomorrow I'll be calling there and going to high school with Lois," she cried. "I knew her home would be lovely but I never dreamed that anything could be so marvelous as this!"

"Yes," agreed Horace enthusiastically, "it is by far the nicest place in Farringdon."

The car went by all too quickly for Judy and for a few minutes more they drove past beautiful homes. Then, as suddenly as they had come upon beauty they came upon ugliness. The pavement ceased abruptly and Grove Street turned and went up hill. A black, muddy road only about half as wide and a broken sidewalk with tall weeds almost covering it, had taken the place of the wide-paved street with a beautiful flower-bed park running through the center.

On the lower side of the black road was an

old factory with broken windows and a caved-in roof. Just above this was an evil-smelling swamp that had been used as a public dump. On the upper side of the road a row of houses, all exactly alike and all painted yellow, stood on a high bank and flight after flight of rickety steps led up to them. In almost every front yard clothes lines full of clothes, some white and some not so white, fluttered in the breeze. Judy set her lips tight together. She had not realized what it meant to be poor in a small city.

"This is what people call 'upper Grove Street,'" Horace remarked with a grimace. "Dad, we're not going to live up here?"

"Not if I can help it," replied the doctor. "Horace, can you see the numbers? We must have passed our house. It couldn't be one of these."

"It must be that one on the corner just before the street turns up hill. These numbers are too high."

When Judy saw the house on the corner she forgot all the ugliness they had passed and stared in fascination. The eye-like windows in the gable ends made it look almost alive but these two round holes were not the only things that gave it that appearance. The house was large and rambling with a wide porch that extended nearly around it. At either end of the porch lattice work reflected moving shadows and a hollow tree, split nearly in half, leaned toward the roof. A tall hedge, badly in need of trimming, surrounded the yard which was overgrown with weeds.

"We ought to have the grass cut and the hedge trimmed right away," Dr. Bolton remarked as he climbed out of the car.

Together they began unloading the suitcases. Blackberry's crate was hoisted onto the porch and Judy carried the kitten inside the house. She needed no key as the door was already open.

The rooms were not what one could call empty, for old newspapers, magazines, leaves, playing cards and cigarette butts littered all the floors. Blackberry was enjoying his freedom and frolicking with scraps of paper.

"Unload those brooms, Horace," Judy called. "I'll need to clear out a place to put things."

"Good heavens!" exclaimed her brother as

he appeared at the door. "Isn't it awful?"

"Never mind," his sister answered, "I'll sweep it out, clean as can be and make a bonfire in the back yard when I'm through."

The idea had occurred to her that perhaps a person might find something in such a litter and if there was anything to be found she wanted to be the one to find it. Apparently Horace had the same idea for he insisted on helping and now and then she noticed him cramming things into his pockets. His actions were mysterious and he refused to tell what he was saving.

When the rooms were finally cleaned, a large green coat button, a brass thimble, a stack of old magazines and a pair of mismated gloves were Judy's reward. Hardly enough to repay her for her trouble, but she decided to keep them as possible clues. Afterwards they made the fire and Horace looked unusually happy as he helped.

The neighbors beyond them in the row all came out on their porches and in their yards and watched the whole proceeding. One short, stumpy woman nodded vigorously to another and both of them started in the direction of the haunted house. Dr. Bolton spoke to them kindly but they were too excited to make any kind of a polite reply.

"We seen ye movin' in," began the older one, "an' figured that mebbe you didn't know this house is hanted."

"Yes, we did know it was supposed to be," spoke up Horace. "But we're not afraid."

"Not afraid?" cried the other woman. "Be ye crazy? Why, folks has seen an' heard sech things o' nights. Ghosts a-talkin' with human voices, callin' 'hello' to them what passes by; screechin's an' screamin's an' scratchin's an' rappin's. Why, we're afeared to look up at them two round winders. Ghosts rise up out o' nothin' an' wave their bony arms at folks. Three famblys moved in an' out o' there in two weeks time an' nobody's lived there since— but we've been after seein' lights flash on an', off 'most every night."

Horace grinned knowingly at his sister and she squeezed his hand. "It *is* true then," she cried, "there will be a mystery to solve and maybe our ghost party will be a—a revelation."

The two old women from the row gasped, opened their mouths but said nothing. Then they turned and almost ran back to tell their neighbors what the strange new people had said.

They were not the only callers who tried to scare away the Bolton family. Early in the evening, after the doctor and Mrs. Bolton had returned from the second trip and they had almost finished cleaning the rooms, Judy heard somebody rapping.

She dropped her mop and almost fell over her mop pail in her hurry to reach the door. This new life in Farringdon promised all kinds of excitement.

There on the porch stood three girls about her own age or a little older. Their faces were older.

"My mother's been telling us," began the tallest one, "that you folks are either awful brave or——"

"She said 'or crazy,'" interrupted the youngest girl, "but we think you're brave."

"That's nice of you," replied Judy. "Won't you come in?"

"Oh, no, thanks!" They seemed very much alarmed at the suggestion. "We'd rather sit here on the porch if you don't mind."

"Not at all," laughed Judy. "Maybe you can tell me some more about the ghosts who are supposed to live here. We haven't heard an unnatural noise all day and I must confess I'm curious to find out why people think the house is haunted."

"We were curious too—once," said the tallest girl in a hushed voice. "Me and Sally and Irene started to stay here one night. Honestly if you could have heard what we heard—but you will," she added with a wise nod of her head.

Irene, the youngest one, then said her bit. "I wasn't scared at first—just noises like rats, but then we heard something cry and something else call out 'Hello Stranger,' life-like, the way old Vine Thompson used to call out to men that went by in the street. Only it was more of a screech. All three of us heard it and we ran for dear life. I wished afterwards I had stayed long enough to see what it was."

"You did see," put in Sally. "Didn't we all see that ghost in the attic window?"

Judy shivered with excitement. "Oh, girls, I'm going to have such fun finding out what it is. Just wait and see."

"I think," ventured Irene, "that I wouldn't be afraid if I were with somebody that wasn't. I'd just as soon come in to your house if you were there."

"I hope you will some time," answered Judy. "Perhaps you can help us. You see," she added with a bright smile, "my brother and I intend to investigate every noise we hear. You say there is a voice——"

"Vine Thompson's voice," Sally interrupted breathlessly. "It's her spirit that haunts the place, crying for revenge."

"Is she dead?" Judy asked in alarm.

"Sure she's dead. I told you that voice was her spirit. It's all very well to be brave," Sally went on, "but when you're dealing with spirits it's another matter. Things happen——"

"What things?"

"You disappear."

Judy could not suppress a smile. It all sounded so absurd—spirits, voices, ghosts, disappearances——

"Laugh if you want to," Sally retorted. "But it's true. We all saw it with our own eyes. Her youngest son went into that house and he never came out again. You must have read it in the papers. Police hunting all over for him, but they can't find him. No wonder. His mother's carried him off to the land of spirits. The voice said so—and," she added in a hoarse whisper, "we three girls heard it."

"Who was this Vine Thompson?" Judy asked, her curiosity fully aroused.

"What! Don't you know?" The three girls turned astonished eyes at her. It was fully a minute before any of them spoke and then Irene said in a tremulous voice. "She—she was murdered. Somebody shot her."

"Shot her!" exclaimed Judy. "Was she killed in our house?"

"Yes, and the strange part of it is that it is her voice that has scared people away. Sometimes I think Sally's right and it is her spirit."

Judy was actually trembling when the three girls left. She tossed her head and smoothed back her hair with a swift motion of her hand. She had resolved not to be frightened and here she was, shaking like a leaf before she had even so much as seen or heard a thing.

She went into the house and turned on all the lights. Everything looked warm and cheerful. They had accomplished much in a few hours. Already the place was beginning to look like home and the new furniture was in keeping with the quiet color of the walls.

"How silly I am," Judy said to herself. "Nothing could happen here."

But when the door bell rang she jumped nervously and then made a firm resolution not to let anything unnerve her again.

It was Irene who had rung the bell and she was standing by the door, a timid little figure in a faded blue coat.

"I'm sorry if we frightened you," she said, "and I almost forgot to tell you what I came to say. There's a young man boarding at our house and he hasn't paid his bills for weeks. He asked me to see if I couldn't get him a job trimming hedges and cutting grass. He seemed very anxious to work for you. We need the money and he needs the work, so if you would——"

"I'll ask Dad," Judy promised. and called him in.

CHAPTER IV

THE CRYING GHOST

"THE neighbors are certainly doing their best to scare us," Horace remarked after Irene had left. He had heard only a part of the conversation on the porch.

"And," added Judy, "the ghosts seem real enough to them. By the way, Donald Carter's story hooks up with what Irene says and I don't believe he made it up after all. I am anxious to explore that attic where everybody has seen a ghost. If you hear any unnatural voices calling, please let me know."

"I will," Horace assured her as he started up the stairs. He was tired and meant to have a good night's rest, ghosts or no ghosts. His new bed had been moved upstairs, but Judy was to sleep on a cot downstairs until her furniture was chosen and the room she had picked out for her own had a better cleaning. This room was the one through the ceiling of which was the hole that led to the attic. She had chosen that particular room on purpose.

In the process of cleaning the front room Judy had found a few more old magazines that looked as if they contained interesting stories. These she had saved to read. She sat down and opened one of them but had no more than glanced at the first page when she heard Horace calling.

"Judy! I do hear something. Come on up-stairs."

At the top of the stairs she stood still and listened. "Rats," she whispered. "Big ones. I thought there'd be rats."

"But rats don't cry," insisted Horace. "Listen!"

Judy stood perfectly still but heard nothing except the scrambling and scratching that she had heard before.

"Call it," suggested Horace.

"How silly!" But just the same Judy called as if she were speaking to a dog. Then again she listened.

A faint cry, like the wailing of a new born baby, answered her call. She heard it again and again, plaintive and small as if something were being hurt. It was not a frightening cry. Instead it aroused Judy's sympathy.

"Poor ghost!" she said aloud. "Horace, it must be something very tiny to cry like that."

But her brother did not answer. The hero of the Roulsville flood stood there with his mouth open and his face had gone white.

"Wake up, silly!" cried his sister, more sharply, perhaps, because her own nerves were on edge. "I thought you were going to help solve this mystery, and there you stand! Be yourself, Horace."

"I—I am being myself," he faltered. "I guess I am a sissy after all."

"Oh no, you aren't." Judy had learned how to manage this brother of hers. "You're just tired. Let's forget about the ghost and once you're asleep you won't hear it any more. Be quiet, Ghost!" she shouted up to the ceiling. "Tomorrow we'll tend to you, but tonight we want to sleep."

Another five minutes of quiet and Judy went downstairs.

"You silenced him all right," Horace called after her. "I guess I'll leave the ghosts to you."

"Oh, no, you won't," she called back, "we're going to have some fun with them, both of us," and to herself she added doubtfully, "but that cry sounded so pitiful."

The next morning Horace appeared to have rested well and nothing more was said about the crying ghost. Dr. and Mrs. Bolton, who had slept downstairs, had not heard it and Judy had other things on her mind. She had dressed herself in the nicest school clothes she owned, and polished her shoes until they shone. She had tied her white blouse at the neck with a red ribbon thinking that it would be a match for her ruby ring. She wanted Lois to notice that she wore it.

Shortly after eight o'clock she left the house without one backward glance at the eye-like windows or at the neighbors in the row who stood staring and wondering. The Boltons were the first family to stay all night in the haunted house since old Vine Thompson died there.

The turrets of Lois' home showed over the tree tops and Judy felt her heart beat faster as she approached the gate. Slowly, she pushed it open and found herself on a gravel pathway that led past flower beds and trees straight up to the palatial door of the Farringdon dwelling. She rang the bell and as she awaited an answer, stood there watching the fountain playing in the morning sunshine. To think that *this* was the home of her best friend!

A colored maid in a white cap and apron opened the door. Judy had never seen a negro except in pictures and this one fascinated her, the dark eyes, the shining teeth as she assured her that Miss Lois would be ready in a minute and asked her to step inside. She felt almost afraid to tread on the heavy oriental rugs.

Lois came in the room directly. She smiled to see her friend admiring her home with wide-eyed amazement.

"Do you like it?" she asked.

"It's — it's — su*per*lative," gasped Judy, hardly knowing whether or not she had used the right word to convey such a world of splendor. Never had she seen anything that could begin to compare with it.

Lois took her arm. "It is nice, isn't it?" she said. "But there are no mysteries about it and no ghosts. Did you——"

"Yes, I did." Judy could not wait for her

friend to finish the question. "It sounded like rats at first and then like a baby crying. I want you to come as soon as you can and help me find out what it is. I'm sure it's in the attic."

"So every one says." Lois told her that she had been inquiring about the house and found it to be full of mysteries.

"And," she added impressively, "Donald Carter really did hear a voice. He was over last night and said again that he would swear to it."

"That's what the mill girls say too."

"What mill girls?" Lois demanded in none too friendly a tone. "Judy, you weren't talking to the mill girls?"

"Why not? They are our neighbors, you know. You see, the house is right on the dividing line between the nice section of Grove Street and the part they call 'upper Grove Street' where the factory workers live."

"That's all the more reason why you should be careful of your associates. Suppose you were classed as one of the mill girls. You wouldn't have a single friend in High School."

Judy stared at her. "Lois Farringdon-Pett,

do you mean to tell me that just because I treat a few poor girls like human beings, all of your crowd will turn me down?"

"Not exactly. Of course I wouldn't," Lois hastened to say. "We've made a pledge but the other girls don't know you as well as I do. They can only judge by what they see— and hear. Please, Judy, for my sake, keep away from those mill girls. They're not our kind."

She had taken her arm and turned off on a quiet side street. A park ran through the center of this street also, but the houses were somewhat smaller and newer. Judy found it hard to decide which street she liked best. This one was so cozy and homelike.

"Is this the way to school?" she asked in surprise.

"No," replied Lois as she paused in front of a dear little stucco house with flowers all around it. "This is Lorraine's house. I always call for her. Maybe you had better wait outside."

Judy could not see why until later. Lorraine appeared at the door, glanced at Judy and assured Lois that it would be all of half an hour before she would be ready. "But I'll wait for you after school," she called as her friend started back down the steps.

"That's funny," mused Lois. "Lorraine always starts early."

Judy, quick to feel an injury, walked on in silence. Arthur had been right about Lorraine's determination not to be friendly and Judy could see where trouble was in store for her. How, she asked herself, could Lois be her best friend and Lorraine's too? The one way out, of course, was for all three of them to be friends. The haunted house, the ghost party Judy was planning and the possible discovery of the stolen jewels were all means to this end.

CHAPTER V

AT THE next turning they came in sight of Girls' High School, a big, modern, four-story brick building. They were early and so Lois had time to show her friend around before she registered at the office.

Afterwards a monitor led her to the study hall where there were seats for three hundred pupils. Judy was given books and a program. On account of moving early in September she had missed about a week's work and soon learned that there were many lessons to be made up.

Kay Vincent, a girl with sleek chestnut hair and cold blue eyes, was asked by the history teacher to lend Judy her notebook. There were five pages of history notes to be copied that night. Judy wished she could have borrowed Lois' notebook instead, but Lois sat at the back of the study hall and the girls who sat near Judy in the front seats were not at

39

all friendly. When whispering was permitted and she attempted to ask a strange girl about the many things that puzzled her, she was promptly told to turn around.

Judy had brought two sandwiches and a slice of cake for lunch but discovered that nearly all the rest of the girls went home for theirs. So, instead of waiting in the empty study hall, she found her way to a nearby furniture store and chose the things she wanted for her room.

A tall man with a flashy green suit waited on her and helped her select just what she liked best. But when she told him the address he seemed less friendly.

"Sure you're going to stay, Miss?" he asked.

"Certainly," she replied. "We've spent one night there already."

"See that this furniture's paid for before it's moved in," he cautioned her. "The store is not responsible for it after that."

"It will be paid for just as soon as it is delivered," she replied and hurried out of the store. She had taken more time than she had intended.

She entered the study hall about two minutes before the bell rang and hailed Lois.

"Do you want to help investigate this ghost business tonight?" she whispered. "Then we'll have something thrilling to tell the girls tomorrow morning. Come home with me after school——"

"But I promised Lorraine——"

Then the bell for classes and more lessons so different from the ones in which she had excelled back in Roulsville. Everyone had been friendly there but here the girls all eyed her critically. Judy had never seemed stupid before. Perhaps it was Kay Vincent's unkind staring at her that made her blunder so in her lessons. By the end of the day Judy was on the verge of tears.

If Lois had been waiting to walk home with her, Judy could have borne it better. Farringdon was a strange city and they had come along so many side streets that Judy could not remember the way home. Perplexed and unhappy, she walked in an uncertain direction as groups of laughing girls passed by without even so much as looking her way.

Suddenly a touch on her arm caused her to jump with surprise and there beside her stood Peter Dobbs.

"Well! Well! Well!" he exclaimed. "If it isn't Judy Bolton, the headless horseman of Dry Brook Hollow. What's gone wrong now, young lady? I believe I see tears in those gray eyes."

Judy laughed as she brushed the tears away. "Not now, Peter. How does it happen that you always appear just when you're needed most? Remember how you picked me up that day when I fell off Ginger and spilled my blackberries?"

"I sure do. How's Blackberry, named for the occasion?"

"Oh, Blackberry's being a good cat and growing up sleek and fat like his mother."

"Sounds as if things were all honey and pie," Peter observed with a perplexed frown. "You're living in Farringdon, I take it, and going to high school. Then why the tears?"

"It's—it's—" Judy faltered. "Oh, I don't know. High school isn't at all like it was in Roulsville. My nerves are all upset."

"Your nerves!" Peter laughed at that. "The idea! Judy Bolton, of all people to be talking about nerves. Why, I thought you weren't afraid of anything."

"I'm not afraid of anything," she declared, "unless—unless it's being unpopular. I want people to like me."

"People do."

Peter said it so seriously that Judy began to giggle. And all the time he was walking along toward home with her until, at last, she knew where she was.

"But," he insisted, "I'm going to take you right to the door."

"That's where we live," she said, and pointed out the house proudly to her companion. "Isn't it spooky looking?"

Peter stood staring at it for fully a minute before he answered.

"So *that's* where you live, is it? Why, I've heard all kinds of tales about that house, tales that would make your hair curl. Donald Carter stayed here one night with a bunch of boys. That was about three weeks ago and he swears he heard old Vine Thompson's voice telling them to clear out. It was her voice only more shrill and rasping. He says it didn't sound human.''

"Well," laughed Judy, "a ghost's voice wouldn't.''

She wasn't going to appear afraid before Peter Dobbs, of all people.

"And," he continued, "another fellow says he heard her call out 'Good morning, stranger,' as he was passing by the house—after she was dead, mind you.''

"I've heard that story too," replied Judy who refused to be sufficiently impressed. "And if I heard a voice calling 'Good morning, stranger' I'd call back, 'stranger yourself!' and ask it what it wanted.''

"Oh, yes, I'll bet you would!" scoffed Peter.

"I'll bet I would too," she retorted. "I did hear a ghost last night and I spoke to it in a stern tone of voice and told it to hush *and it did.*''

"It did, eh?''

"Yes, it did." Judy stood still, watching the attic windows, her saucy nose tilted toward the sky.

"Horace and I are going to solve all kinds of

mysteries before we've been here long," she went on. "I'll be an expert on ghosts and I can do it too because I'm not afraid."

"And have folks told you about the strange noises, lights flashing off and on——"

"Yes, and screechings and howlings and rappings. Don't you know that up in that round attic window—a—ghost—is—supposed—to—appear?"

Peter and Judy were both staring at what they both believed must be some trick of their eyesight. In the eye-like attic window something white rose slowly, stretched its skinny arms, and slowly disappeared below the sill.

Three times they saw it, white against the blackness behind it, and three times they gasped and stared first at what they had seen and then at each other.

CHAPTER VI

MORE MYSTERIES

"Judy, did you see what I saw?" asked Peter Dobbs after a breathless silence.

"I certainly saw something," she replied, still trembling. "Oh, Peter, here comes Horace just too late. Won't he be astonished when we tell him?"

Horace was more than astonished. His face turned almost as white as the ghost's face as he listened to the weird tale that Judy and Peter had to tell. Anyone could see that he was frightened and plainly he was trying to laugh it off as he said, "Well, Peter, it looks as if we were in for a little excitement before we solve this mystery but," and there was determination in his voice, "we are not going to be scared away, not just yet at any rate."

"I should say not," agreed Judy, "not with a Halloween party in the air. The more excitement the better. If there weren't any ghosts there wouldn't be any mystery and if

46

we can prove they are fakes we can have bushels of fun showing them up.''

"Quite an idea!" laughed Peter. "Your head seems to be full of ideas and if you are the one who is getting up this party you speak of I'm sure it will be jolly. Remember, I want an invitation.''

"You'll get one," Judy assured him, "you and your mother——''

"My mother?''

"Oh, your grandmother, I mean. I don't know why, but I always think of Mrs. Dobbs as your mother.''

"Well," confessed Peter, "she is all the mother I know anything about.''

Judy had always wondered about Peter's parents. This seemed to be a good opportunity to question him on the subject.

"Did your real mother die when you were a baby?'' she asked.

"I don't know. Why?''

"Well, just because I wondered. You're not adopted, are you?''

"Look here, Judy," Peter answered sharply, "this question of parents is—is—well, rather delicate. I tell you I don't know anything about my mother. I don't know whether Mrs. Dobbs is my grandmother or not, although people do say I look like her. We have the same light blue eyes and blunt noses and her hair used to be blonde before it got so white. I've tried to get her to talk about it but she just looks hurt and says nothing. I mentioned the matter once to Granddad and he got mad. 'Aren't you getting good care?' he demanded, 'that you must be looking for better folks than we are?' I was quite a youngster then, but I've never dared ask about my parents since. So you see, Judy,'' he added more gently, ''We all have our troubles.''

''Yes,'' she agreed, ''and, as Dad once told me, we must 'grin and bear them.' But sometimes it is dreadfully hard to grin.''

She told Horace just how hard it had been that day in school.

''Everybody's so cold and distant—and so proper. I don't believe those girls have any feelings.''

Horace made a good listener and helped solve the problem of school supplies by buying them himself. He walked part way home with Peter Dobbs and bought them at a stationery store.

"That boy does seem worried," Horace re-
marked to his sister when he had returned. "I
wish we could do something to help him find
out who his folks are. A boy has a right to
know."

"Yes," she agreed, "and Mr. and Mrs. Dobbs
are so lovely. I can't understand their actions
toward Peter at all. If he is an adopted boy I
should think he would call them 'mother' and
'father' and if they really are his grandparents
I certainly can't see why he shouldn't know it.
Horace, do you suppose Dad would know any-
thing about it?"

"He might. The Dobbs family have lived in
Roulsville as far back as I can remember."

"Anyway I think I'll ask Mrs. Dobbs her-
self," Judy decided. "I know she is fond of
me and maybe I can think of some clever way
to put the question. Here, Horace, let me have
that loose leaf notebook at the bottom of the
stack." He was still holding her school sup-
plies. "I have five pages of history notes to
copy after supper. I wish you'd help me with
this algebra too. I can't understand what X
stands for."

"All sorts of problems to solve, aren't

there?'' he laughed. Most of them would prob-
ably be more difficult than a sum in algebra.

Judy had not expected her furniture to be
delivered until the following day but, when they
reached the house, she was delighted to find
the men already moving it into her room.

''They seemed worried for fear we wouldn't
pay for it,'' her mother said. ''So I had to give
them cash right away. They wouldn't even ac-
cept a check. Judy, didn't you tell them who
you were?''

''Certainly, Mother. They acted worried
about the money this noon too. Seemed to
think the furniture might vanish over night.
Did I spend too much?''

Mrs. Bolton assured her that she was a
splendid shopper and offered to help arrange
the curtains and rugs in her bedroom before
dinner. Judy had even remembered to buy a
lavender cushion to match her curtains and
spread. This was for Blackberry's daytime
naps. She had bought a desk which was placed
beside the window for her studying and, best
of all, a dresser with a secret drawer. The
drawer locked under a panel and, when closed,

appeared to be only a strip of decorative moulding.

Judy tried her new chair and it felt so soft and comfortable that she sat there for a while looking out of the window. Something was moving behind the hedge.

In another moment Judy was laughing at herself for being so nervous. It was only the man Irene had told them about and he had just finished trimming the hedge. She saw him sweep the cut leaves into a neat pile at the curb. He glanced about furtively and then began ascending the hollow tree in front of the house. What was he doing? Judy opened the window and called.

"Prune the tree, Miss," he called back. But she noticed that he had neither an axe nor a saw.

"You can't prune the tree with those hedge shears," she told him sharply. "I'll see if Dad won't give you your money and let you quit for the day."

"Thank you, Miss."

The man looked sheepish and climbed awkwardly down from the tree.

Judy left her pretty room reluctantly and called her father. Nothing was said about the tree but the man seemed pleased with his pay and walked off counting the bills and muttering something under his breath.

That evening Judy was anxious to begin her lessons at her pretty new desk. Her shaded lamp shed a rosy glow over her books and she decided to finish her note copying. She produced Kay Vincent's neatly written work and proceeded to duplicate it as near as she was able although her handwriting had a characteristic slant that prevented it from looking as neat as Kay's precise penmanship. She had completed the first three pages and her pen scratched away on the fourth page louder and louder.

"What a scratchy pen," she thought. It was disconcerting when she was trying her best to hurry. She stopped writing for a minute but could still hear the scratching sound.

"It isn't my pen," she said in alarm. "It's that noise in the attic again."

She stood up and listened and could hear the same plaintive cry that she had heard the night before. It sounded less like a baby this time.

Maybe it was only a bat. Judy had heard of bats squeaking and that dismal attic would be an ideal place for a bat to live.

"Mmmmmmmmmm!"

No, it wasn't a bat after all.

"Horace!" she called. "Horace! Is there a ladder anywhere around? No? Then come up here and bring some boxes. I'm going to climb up and find out what's in that attic."

In a minute more her brother had arrived, his arms stacked with packing boxes. There had been plenty of them left over from moving.

"Pile them up," directed Judy, "and I'll climb up—or you can, if you'd rather."

"No—no—" he stammered. "I—that is, I will if you want me to."

"Never mind. You'll have to hold the boxes. Now don't get scared and let me fall. I may have to do some pushing before that cover swings off the opening. I suppose you do push it to open it."

"I suppose so," he answered. "Here, can you climb up all right?"

Judy was already climbing and stood, not very securely, on top of the wabbly pile. She reached up with both hands and pushed, but the door to the opening stuck and would not give way. Horace helped with the broom handle and after five minutes of pushing and banging the queer little door in the ceiling creaked and opened. The flat cover fell back with a loud bang and at the same time Judy saw a flash of something white. She gave a startled cry, lost her balance and, boxes and all, crashed in a heap on the floor.

"Why didn't you hold it?" she screamed at her brother.

"I tried to. But I couldn't steady it very well when I had the broom. Judy, are you hurt?" he inquired anxiously as he helped her to her feet. Her knee was bleeding and he wrapped his clean handkerchief around it. But she had received an ugly cut and the handkerchief was soon stained red.

"Better let Dad take care of it," Horace suggested.

Accordingly they went together down to their father's office where he was busily arranging his medical equipment. He had just assembled a white operating table to be used for all minor operations and for dressing severe wounds.

Judy mounted the table and held her bruised knee for her father to see.

"Your first patient in Farringdon," she teased him. "Will I need an anesthetic?"

"Chloroform, probably," the doctor replied with a twinkle of his sympathetic gray eyes. They were like his daughter's and he understood this vivacious auburn-haired girl better than she understood herself.

"I can tell without asking that you have been doing some investigating. Where? In the attic?"

"Yes, Dad. We climbed up on packing boxes. I saw something white——"

Horace interrupted her with an exclamation of awe.

"You didn't tell me!"

"I fell before I had a chance," she replied. "You see, it—it startled me a little."

"I should think it would."

"But I'm not afraid," she declared resolutely. "Only the next time we will stack the boxes up more carefully."

They heard the doctor chuckling to himself as they left the office. He knew they were

investigating but seemed to have no fears.
Judy intended to keep her nerves as steady
as his.

"Now we'll try it again," she announced
cheerfully after she and Horace had finished
piling the boxes into a more substantial
pyramid.

CHAPTER VII

TRACKS

THE opening in the ceiling had been left uncovered. Judy caught hold of the sides of the queer doorway and lifted herself up so that she could peer into the dark attic. Two shafts of light from the two round windows showed her that the attic was, by no means, empty. Boxes, dishes, paper, a trunk and an old bird cage near the window were only a few of the things that she beheld in dim out-line. A floor of rough planks covered only about half of the attic and the place smelled perfectly dreadful.

"Horace," she gasped. "Get me a gas mask. It smells like something dead up here."

"But do you see anything?" he wanted to know.

"Not yet. Nothing except a lot of junk piled up. Oh, this odor is awful. I don't see how a respectable ghost could stand it. I can't stay up here another minute."

"Guess we've both had enough of this un-earthly stuff for tonight," Horace agreed as he took his sister's hand and helped her down from the pile of boxes.

It was getting late and Judy had almost for-gotten the task ahead of her. But she had promised Kay Vincent that she would return her notebook in the morning and the History lesson must be finished. She filled her foun-tain pen, wiped the point on a piece of tissue paper and was just about to settle herself to her note copying again when, to her dismay, she noticed that Kay's carefully prepared pages were covered with dirty brown tracks. What could have made them? Judy was too upset to ponder this new mystery. She tried to erase the strange smudges but only suc-ceeded in making the page look worse.

"Horace!" she cried in despair, "come and see what has happened to this notebook. Oh! What shall I do?"

He stared at the tracks in horrified silence. It was apparent that the page was hopelessly blotted but he could think of no solution to the problem.

"Couldn't I copy them all over again?" asked Judy.

"Copy Kay's notes? That would never do. The teachers will not accept notes in any one else's handwriting and you would have a time imitating it. You'll just have to apologize to this girl—Harry Vincent's daughter of all people—and I know how snippy she is."

Judy knew too and that night she lay awake dreading it. The house was so quiet that she could hear Horace breathing in the next room. She could hear something else, a faint rapping which grew increasingly louder as the night wore on.

One—*two*—three. One two. One—*two*—three. One two—as rhythmic as the ticking of a clock. Judy lay there in the dark listening, fearing the ghostly rappings less than she did the disapproval of Kay Vincent, a girl she hardly knew. Finally, long after midnight, she dropped off to sleep, the One—*two*—three still pounding in her brain.

Later, how much later Judy did not know, she awoke suddenly and sat up in bed all atremble. A series of thumps, scrapes and

scratching sounds were issuing from the ceil-
ing. What was worse, the door to the attic
was slightly ajar and she was sure she and
Horace had closed it and fitted it securely into
the opening.

Something strong enough to move the door
must be up there in the attic!

Judy seized her flashlight and moved the bed
over to where she could climb on the head rail
and see. The noise increased suddenly but
by the time Judy had climbed up and was able
to look into the attic everything was quiet. The
circle of light revealed nothing except the
trunk, papers and boxes that she had seen be-
fore. She played the flashlight in every corner
and then, repulsed by the terrific odor, climbed
down with a disappointed sigh.

Whatever was up there seemed to be capa-
ble of disappearing and, Judy reasoned, there
must be a closet or something of the kind for
the creature to hide in. She would climb up
with Horace some other time when there was
plenty of opportunity to make a thorough
search.

The whole thing had unnerved her more than
she realized and, in almost no time, it was

morning. Judy remembered the unpleasant
duty ahead of her. She must apologize to Kay
Vincent for soiling her notebook. How, Judy
wondered, could she possibly explain those
dirty tracks? Kay wouldn't believe her if she
told the truth. Perhaps Lois could suggest a
way out.

But when Judy called at the palatial door
of the Farringdon-Pett dwelling the maid in-
formed her that Miss Lois had left early. She
had probably stopped for Lorraine.

As she walked on toward school Judy con-
soled herself with the thought that Lois might
be in the study hall and, in that case, she could
depend on her to sympathize and help
straighten things out with Kay.

The study hall was almost empty when Judy
arrived. A group of girls were standing in
a far corner talking and laughing. To her
dismay, Judy noticed that one of these girls
was Kay Vincent. Almost immediately she
came forward and demanded her notebook.

Judy had expected Kay's cold stare but was
quite unprepared for what followed.

"You couldn't keep anything clean," Harry
Vincent's daughter stormed. "I might have

known that. Anybody that would live in **Vine** Thompson's dirty house——"

"The house isn't dirty," Judy defended hotly. "We cleaned it thoroughly before we even moved our furniture in."

"You couldn't clean up such a house," said Kay angrily.

"Well," answered Judy angrily, "your father didn't even try. He didn't tell us about that woman who was murdered there either. Who was she anyway?"

Kay's eyes narrowed and she seemed to be looking through, not at Judy.

"If you know about her," she retorted spitefully, "you wouldn't stay in that house another night."

"Is that so?" Judy's cheeks were hot with anger, her eyes red from lack of sleep and altogether she made a most unhappy picture as she stood in the aisle storming at Kay. "If that's the case your father had a lot of nerve offering the house to a hero like my brother. I suppose that was his way of dodging taxes on a place he couldn't rent. But don't worry, it will take more than Vine Thompson's spirit to scare us away from the house and any information I get, Kay Vincent, I won't get from you."

But Harry Vincent's daughter had not heard this outburst of temper. She had left the study hall just as Lois entered and stood in the doorway with a surprised and hurt expression in her brown eyes.

"How could you?" she asked. "Oh, Judy, I'm so disappointed. Perhaps Lorraine was right after all and you are not the kind of girl we want in our group. And I did hope that you would try and be a lady like——"

"Like Kay Vincent, I suppose?" interrupted Judy with anger still in her voice.

"Well, at least Kay says her unkind things in a ladylike way. I don't know what she said but I am sure you could have answered her without losing your temper. That isn't the way to make friends, Judy. It's the way to lose the few friends you have. I've tried to be true to our pledge and treat you just the same as I do Lorraine, but you don't realize how hard you are making it for me."

Judy did realize, suddenly, and hung her head. "I—I'm sorry," she murmured. "It's hard for me too."

That evening Judy went for a walk to think things out alone. This time, instead of walking down Grove Street toward Lois' home, she walked up toward the factory section. The shabby little houses on the hillside looked more cheerful after dark. The shades in Irene's house were pulled to the top and through the lighted window Judy could see her sitting at her piano. She stood for ten or fifteen minutes listening to Irene as she played and sung old time melodies for her father who seemed to be a cripple. His crutch rested beside his chair.

Irene had just closed her piano and turned out the light when Judy realized that she was not standing alone. A man had been standing beside her and now he turned and spoke.

"Nice music, wasn't it?" he said.

"Why, yes, I enjoyed it."

Judy spoke guardedly. She had recognized the voice of the man who had trimmed their hedge and attempted to prune the tree. She was not anxious to engage in a conversation with him, especially on upper Grove Street.

"I'll have to hurry home," she said.

"Wait a minute." The man caught at her

arm. "Don't mind if I walk with you? It's dark along here."

Judy knew it was dark. She glanced fearfully at the deserted factory across the street and then at the man who was quickening his pace to keep step with her. She would have preferred darkness to his company.

"Ain't afraid, are you?"

"Oh, no. But I don't know you. I'd rather walk alone."

"Sure you know me," he insisted. "You're the doctor's daughter. I've been kinda hopin' that your pa would have some more work for me. Ain't there anything you want done inside the house?"

"No. I am sure there isn't. Mother and I take care of that."

"Yeah? How about cleaning the attic? You ain't been up there yet, eh, Miss?"

Judy gave a little start. She could not truthfully say "no" and she dared not say "yes." She was a little worried.

"What makes you think the attic needs cleaning?" she asked.

"Sort of suspicioned it did, that's all. Most women folks don't relish cleanin' dark holes like that 'specially when they're hanted.'

"We'll send for you if you're wanted."

Judy managed to break away from the man and ran up the steps and into the house. Horace met her at the door and she could see that he was worried.

"Who is that man outside?" he wanted to know.

"That fellow who cut the grass," Judy replied as she threw her coat on a chair arm and sank in the chair beside it. "I hope Dad doesn't hire him again. He's altogether too familiar."

"I didn't like his face either," Horace agreed. "Judy, I wish you wouldn't go out alone at night. There are plenty of people who enjoy walking with you. Peter Dobbs, for instance. He was here while you were out, talking about his folks again and seemed anxious about his grandmother. Dad gave him some medicine for her."

"Oh, I wish I had been here." Judy was genuinely disappointed. "Peter didn't say any more about his own folks, his parents, I mean. Did he?"

"Only that he doesn't think his grandparents will ever tell him who they were. He seemed quite certain that they wouldn't answer questions. Funny business, I call it. Judy, I've got a surprise for you."

"Really?"

"Yes, and it's alive. Come on up in your room and see it."

Wondering, she followed him up the stairs

CHAPTER VIII

HORACE'S BLACK NOTEBOOK

"I'LL give you three guesses." Horace paused with his hand on the knob of the door to Judy's room.

"I think it's a watch dog. We really need one, don't we?"

"No. Something smaller than that."

"I know. A globe of goldfish. I've always wanted some to keep on my window sill."

"Wrong again," Horace cried as he swung open the door. "You see, it doesn't go at all well with goldfish."

"Horace! Not another cat!"

Judy was regarding the scrawny white creature curled up on Blackberry's cushion with disapproval.

"He needs a bath," she said at length. "And he looks as if he hadn't eaten a decent meal in weeks. Where did you get him?"

"Found him," Horace replied shortly.

"I thought so. He looks like a stray. Blackberry wouldn't stand for such a dirty intruder lying on his cushion. Look! He's soiled it already.''

"So he has!''

Both of them could see that the cushion was not the same dainty lavender that it had been before. Where the white cat had curled his lean body it had changed to a drab gray.

Blackberry himself had padded up the stairs and stood in the doorway arching his back and eyeing the white intruder with the injured dignity of a king forced to abdicate his throne.

Judy lifted the white cat gingerly and carried him downstairs where, in spite of his yowling protests, he was thrust into a tub of soapy water.

"If we must keep two cats," she declared, "both of them are going to be clean.''

Judy was dousing the kitten with a sponge as she talked and, wet and shivering, he looked more starved than ever. Afterwards she dried him with a Turkish towel and gave him a saucer of warm milk. Then, much to his humiliation, Blackberry was put outside and his cushion given over to the half-grown white cat.

"I'll get a new cushion for Blackberry."

Judy announced, "and really, Horace, if you don't mind, I think this white skeleton ought to sleep in the hall. He doesn't fit in with the color scheme in my room."

"What would you want, a purple cat? It suits me, though. In fact," Horace continued with an amused smile, "since you don't appreciate my gift, I think I'll keep the white cat myself. I've even thought of a good name for him, 'The Ghost.' How do you like it?"

"It suits him," Judy agreed. "I never in all my life saw such a scrawny creature."

Horace had found a place in a corner of his own room for the soiled lavender cushion and was stroking the cat who answered with a loud crackling purr.

"It sounds as if he had asthma," Judy said in disgust. "You really ought to give him some medicine. Maybe Dad can suggest something."

"I'll ask him," Horace promised and seated himself beside the table where he usually did his writing. He sat there thoughtfully tapping on his chin with the end of his pencil. That and the sound of the kitten's harsh purring grated on Judy's nerves.

"You're certainly a help," she remarked with a shrug. "You were going to investigate all the noises we heard and here you are only making them worse."

"You wanted to live in a haunted house," he charged, looking up with a provoking smile. "Remember, sis, it's all your idea and a ghost and a black cat add something to the spookiness of the place. Why, I saw one of those old women from the row run half a block to keep Blackberry from crossing her path."

Horace was still chuckling over this when Judy left the room and settled herself at her own desk to finish her homework.

"One—*two*—three.   One two.   One—*two*—three.   One two," sounded the ghostly rappings on the wall.   Judy found herself making one blunder after the other as she pursued her lessons.   She almost wished she had been sensible and chosen the quiet room across the hall. Finally she closed her books in desperation, thrust them under her arm and marched into Horace's room.

"You'll have to let me study in here with you," she announced.   "I can't stand that room of mine another minute.   Do you mind putting that cat out so we can have half an hour's peace?"

"Not at all."

He lifted the scrawny creature, cushion and all, and removed it to the farthest end of the hall. When he returned he stood in the doorway regarding his sister with a perplexed frown. This irritable person did not seem like the same girl who had been so thrilled with the idea of living in a haunted house that she had chosen the most perilous room on purpose.

"What's the matter?" he asked. "Did you hear something?"

"Please, Horace," she begged, "leave me alone until I'm finished with these equations and then if you insist we will get busy on the mysteries."

"I am busy on them." He exhibited a small black notebook. "What do you suppose is in here?"

"I haven't the remotest idea. What?"

"Ghost stories," he replied with a grin. He then pocketed the notebook and would talk no more of it.

"Well, if he's so good at solving mysteries," Judy said to herself the following night when

she attempted to do some studying in her room,
"he ought to be interested in this one.
Horace!" she called. "Come here and listen
to this!"

He bounded up the stairs and paused in the
doorway, his head cocked to one side and a
comical expression on his face. "One—*two*—
three. One two. One—*two*—three. One two"
sounded the weird rappings. This time, to
Judy's amazement, her brother did not seem at
all frightened but took out his black notebook
and jotted down something, then tucked it away
in his pocket again and told his sister that the
mystery would soon be solved.

"Detective Bolton is now on the job for fair,"
he said with a flourish of his pencil, "and a
master of mysteries is he."

Judy did not return to her studying directly,
but went over to the secret drawer in her
dresser where she kept her clues.

"Perhaps they aren't as interesting as his,"
she said to herself. "But we shall see who is a
'Master of Mysteries.'"

However, a whole week-end passed without
any investigating or further exploring of the
attic. Instead, Horace and Judy called on the

Dobbs family after a quiet morning at church. They sat in the parlor of the neat little apartment that took the place of the big white house where they used to live in Roulsville. The apartment was furnished less expensively but in good taste.

The nice old couple were glad to see their hero and his sister and Mrs. Dobbs' blackberry tarts were an especial treat. They reminded Judy of the blackberry jam that the kind old lady had once purchased from her. That jam, like all the rest of their belongings, had been washed away in the Roulsville flood.

All the time Judy sat visiting she kept wanting to ask about Peter's mother. The boy, himself, was not there and it seemed to be a splendid opportunity to find out things.

"Peter says he looks like you, Mrs. Dobbs," she began, "but I don't think he looks very much like either you or his grandfather."

"Indeed!" The old lady smiled. "He's a fine looking boy at any rate, so we're not worrying where he gets his good looks."

"Perhaps from his own father or mother," suggested Judy timidly.

Mr. Dobbs jumped to his feet. "The boy

looks like his grandmother,'' he cried, and to make the statement more impressive he punctuated it with a hard thump on the table. ''It's his grandmother's eyes he's got and her nose and her hair and her complexion. There isn't any doubt of it.''

There was absolute silence for several minutes after that. Then Mr. Dobbs asked more civilly, ''Well, how's high school, Judy? I reckon you're at the head of the class again.''

''Not now,'' she explained, ''but I'm catching up. Languages aren't so easy, but I love English composition and math. I'm taking six subjects. That's all we're allowed to take.''

''And if you were allowed to take ten, by golly, you'd be taking ten,'' chuckled Mr. Dobbs.

From that time on they talked of everything except Peter. The boy came in just as they were preparing to leave and offered to walk home with them.

''Did you ask any questions about my parents?'' he wanted to know as soon as the three young people were alone.

''Tried to,'' answered Horace, ''at least, Judy did, but it didn't work out.''

"Didn't suppose it would," he replied shortly, "but it did no harm to try."

"Your grandfather nearly took my head off," said Judy, "but, of course, there was no harm in that. I'm not used to being handled like a china doll."

Peter chuckled. "A girl that lives in a haunted house ought to be able to stand rough treatment. By the way, did you find out anything about that ghost we saw in the window?"

Judy started to tell him that they hadn't found out a single thing but before she could open her mouth to speak, Horace answered gravely.

"The results of any investigation on the part of the committee are to be withheld until the day of the grand demonstration when all will be divulged and expounded."

"Who was it that read the dictionary?" asked Peter, "you or your sister?"

"I did," laughed Judy, "but he uses the big words oftener. I'll act as an interpreter if necessary."

She found it easier, however, to interpret her brother's words than his actions. Late the next night he took his little black notebook and.

with a pencil over his ear, proceeded to climb the hollow tree in front of the house. Judy watched him as he tapped on the tree with the pencil, broke off twigs here and there and did a few other curious things.

"The committee must not be disturbed," he replied when she endeavored to find out what it was all about.

After she was in bed Judy listened but heard no more rappings. Instead she heard a scraping sound like something being dragged across a bare floor. The rappings had not disturbed her except when she was very tired, but this scraping! It made her shudder.

"Horace!" she called. "I don't think the committee has improved matters much. I never *can* sleep with somebody dragging dead bodies across the floor."

"Horrors!" he exclaimed. "Now what have I done?"

With his black book in one hand and a rope in the other, he dashed out of his room and again ascended the tree.

CHAPTER IX

HIDDEN TREASURE

A STREET lamp overhead made it possible for Horace to see what he was doing, but showed Judy, watching from her bedroom window, only his form in black outline. She saw women in the row watching too, probably believing that Horace was another "hant."

He had tied one end of the rope securely about a branch when suddenly Judy saw him bend over and begin taking things out of the hollow place in the tree, stuffing them into his pockets. This took about ten minutes while Judy, her father and mother downstairs and people in the row all stood staring at him. Then he started tugging away at the rope until he had bound the two sections of the tree tightly together. The scraping sound had ceased, but Judy was no longer interested in that. What had her brother taken out of the tree? She dressed herself hurriedly and ran downstairs to find out.

Horace stood in the center of the kitchen floor, his face pale and his hands trembling.

"It looks as if we were in a mess," he said. "Something funny has been happening in this house and bigger and stronger things than ghosts are responsible for it."

Judy eyed his bulging pockets curiously.

"It does look as if something funny has been happening," she said. "Not in the house but in the tree. Horace, I want to know what's in your pockets."

"Then come away from the window," he whispered excitedly, "and I'll show you. Those rubbering neighbors have seen too much already."

They followed him to a corner of the kitchen where he reached in his pockets and drew out, first a long string of pearls, then two diamond bracelets, three watches, pins with precious stones set in them and a quantity of rings. He dumped them in a glittering heap on the kitchen table where the sauce pans were still turned up to drain.

"Oh, Horace!" exclaimed Judy, her eyes round as saucers. "That's our first real find!"

"We're going to find out who it belongs to

and do that mighty quick," Horace replied in alarm. "If we were caught with all this jewelry we'd be accused of stealing it."

"You're right, Son," said Dr. Bolton. "Better take it along to the police station first thing in the morning."

"Please, Horace," pleaded his sister. "Let me come with you. And can't I take the jewels, just for a minute? I want to look them over."

He stepped to one side of the table and his sister, her face radiant with expectation, reached in among the treasures and examined each ring.

"Are you sure you got all of them out of the tree?" she asked anxiously when she had finished with the pile.

"Pretty sure," he replied. "But I'll go up and look again if you want me to."

"Please do. You see," she explained to her father, "Lorraine Lee lost a friendship ring and I would be the happiest girl in the world if I could find it."

"I'm afraid there's not much chance of it, Judy girl," the doctor said.

"No," Judy agreed. "I suppose there isn't

but I live in hopes. That and Peter Dobbs' parents interest me more than any other puzzles I have ever tried to solve.''

''What about Peter's parents?'' asked the doctor.

Judy had been waiting for an opportunity to discuss the matter with her father and her eyes kindled with interest.

''He says he doesn't know who they are. Dad, can you remember Peter when he was a little boy?''

Dr. Bolton stroked his broad forehead and thought. ''The first time I ever saw him,'' he said at length, ''was when he was about four years old and had the measles. I supposed the Dobbs family had adopted him.''

''They wouldn't be his grandparents then, would they?''

''Hardly,'' the doctor replied, ''but he might call them that. However, I am inclined to agree with you that there is more to this case than we know.''

''Did they ever have any children of their own, Dad?''

''I believe there was a daughter,'' the doctor

remembered. "There were no sons though and the daughter died very young. I never knew the girl."

"Not even her name."

"No," he replied, "not even her name. I'm afraid it's too much of a puzzle, Judy. I wouldn't try to figure it out."

"That's why I like it, Dad, because it's a puzzle. Heavens! has Horace been up the tree all this time?"

They had forgotten him during their conversation. Judy went out on the porch and called softly.

"Coming," he called back. "Sorry, sis, but I couldn't find a thing."

Judy tried not to show her disappointment. It was absurd, she knew, to keep hoping for this solution of her troubles at school.

"What made you stay up in the tree so long?" she asked when he was back in the house again.

Horace hesitated. "You probably won't believe me," he said, "but I would have sworn there was somebody else up in the tree. I heard the branches snap above me and saw a dark something, and then it disappeared."

Judy spent an uneasy night. She had begged Horace to let her keep the jewels and the responsibility of them kept her awake. Noises in the attic disturbed her too and once she thought she saw the small door in the ceiling opening. She sat up in her bed and screamed.

Horace heard her and rushed into the room.

"Judy!" he exclaimed. "What's the matter?"

"Oh, nothing," she replied. "Just some queer noises that woke me suddenly and I screamed before I was quite awake. I think I'll leave the light on the rest of the night."

Horace waited in the room for ten minutes before he left his sister alone again. Then, as they heard no more strange sounds, he went back to his bed and was soon sound asleep.

Before six in the morning the telephone's insistent ring sounded in the hall.

"It's for you, Son," Dr. Bolton called up to Horace presently. "Never mind coming down now. They want you at the newspaper office right away. There's been a robbery down on the south side of town and you have been assigned to report it."

"Dad!" Horace leaped out of bed and Judy, sharing his excitement, knew that further sleep was out of the question. She dressed herself hurriedly and was downstairs in less time than it usually took her to comb her hair.

Horace was already getting his own breakfast and stood at the kitchen table buttering a roll. Judy helped by preparing his coffee and frying two eggs, one of which she ate herself.

"What's your hurry?" he asked between mouthfuls of roll.

"Why, I'm going with you," she exclaimed. "Don't you remember you said I could? You'll have to stop at the police station on the way."

"Oh, bother!" Horace, apparently had forgotten the jewels. "I won't have time. Would you just as soon do it, Judy?"

"Just as soon!" she cried joyfully. "Why, I can't think of anything I'd rather do. This is so thrilling!"

"It will make a thrilling newspaper story too," Horace remarked as he hurried out of the door.

CHAPTER X

AT THE POLICE STATION

WHEN Chief of Police Kelly heard Judy's story first he looked very serious and then went off into peal after peal of loud laughter.

"Can you beat it!" he roared. "What that Vine Thompson wouldn't do to get around the law. She figured she'd leave the loot in the tree until she got her freedom and then go back in the same crooked business again. That's how these criminals work it. No use jailing them. They never learn."

"But I thought she was dead!" Judy exclaimed, staring at the good-natured chief who had listened so attentively to her account of the discovery of the jewels in the hollow tree.

"Sure, and she is dead," he replied. "Her own gang got her in the end. We caught the one who did the killing and three others but the rest of the gang are still at large. Maybe one or two of them, maybe a dozen, but nobody's yet been able to lay hands on her youngest son. He's too clever.''

"What were they? Robbers?" Judy's cheeks were glowing with interest and she meant to find out all she could while she had the chance.

"Sure, every mother's son of 'em. And Vine was the cleverest fence the department had yet run across. Nobody ever found out where she sold the loot. We raided the house and didn't find more than ten dollars' worth of stolen goods in it. But when Vine saw her own game was up she squealed on the robbers. No pity in her heart, not even for her sons. One of them was leader of the gang. He's in the pen for life along with the man who shot her.''

"Oh! They arrested the man who shot her?''

"And why not? He confessed with his own lips.''

"It was just what some of the factory girls told me about her spirit crying for revenge. Of course it's superstition but I thought maybe the man who killed her was at large.''

"Oh! Ho!" the chief chuckled. "So you've been hearing tales too. 'Spose you know your house is said to be haunted?''

"Said to be?" Judy was thinking of the noises that had awakened her the night before. "It is more than that, Chief Kelly. There really are the most curious noises in the attic but every time we look up there the—the things that make the strange sounds disappear."

"I believe you," Chief Kelly answered seriously. "The wonder to me is that you folks have been able to stick it out as long as you have. But listen here, young lady, if you ever catch sight of anybody prowling around the place or trying to get in the windows, let me know, won't you? But understand now, that doesn't mean shadows. The Department hasn't any time for fooling around with ghosts."

"I see." Judy studied the chief's face quizzically. Just how serious was he, she wondered. Well, at any rate, he would be a dependable person to call on if that man who tried to prune the tree made himself unpleasant again.

"I'm interested in Vine Thompson," she said presently. "Tell me some more about her. Were both of her sons robbers?"

"Three sons she had," the chief answered, "and all three of them went wrong in one way or another. The oldest one was killed and the second one, as I told you, is in the penitentiary. The third son is the cagiest one of the lot——"

"He's the one who disappeared in our house," Judy interrupted.

"Who said so?" the chief inquired brusquely.

"Oh, one of those factory girls. Said she and some other girls saw him go into the house and never come out again. They were sure that his mother's spirit had carried him off."

"Humph!" Chief Kelly exclaimed. "That's a new one on me. When did this happen?"

"I'm not sure," Judy replied. "But it must have been after our house was empty."

For a while after that the room was perfectly quiet except for the tapping of the chief's finger on the side of his pipe. He was figuring out something, Judy thought, and so she waited for him to speak.

"Wal," he drawled at length, "it's beginning to look as if there was more to this ghost business than just superstition. Those jewels you people found prove that much. And I've been laying a good many robberies at the door of Vine's son who is still at large. This one last night for instance."

"I know," Judy broke in. "My brother has gone to report it for the *Herald*."

"Yeah?" The chief sat forward in his swivel chair. "Your brother is a reporter, is he? I suppose he's let it out already about these jewels in the tree. If we could only keep that hushed up we might catch the rest of Vine's gang."

"Oh, if we only could!" Judy's eyes were big with excitement. "I might call him up before he puts in the story——"

"Fine, girlie. I wish you would." He handed her the telephone.

"Herald Office?" she inquired when the operator had given her the correct number. "May I speak to Horace Bolton?"

"He's out. No. He just came in this very minute, but he is busy now. Won't you call back later?" the voice at the other end of the wire asked. Judy insisted that her message was important and Horace was finally called.

"What is it, Judy? Any more news?"

"Plenty," she replied, "but if you want a good big front page story later on you'll have to keep quiet about those jewels you found. The Chief of Police said so."

"Why, yes, er——"

"What's the matter?" Judy demanded impatiently. "Have you already told them?"

"No, not the paper. I—I— Wait a minute," he delayed her. "I'll take your call from the booth where I can talk better. There! No, Judy. I haven't told them here at the office. In fact, I only told one person and I'm sure that can't make any difference. He's only a little boy."

"Little boys talk. Who was it?"

"Dickie Vincent."

"Kay's little brother! Good night!" exclaimed Judy. "You might as well have put it on a bulletin board."

"I'm sorry, sis. I didn't know."

"But you won't put it in the paper," she begged.

"No, of course not. I've got a story that will fill a good column on the front page," he added proudly. "Those people who were robbed saw the burglars and gave me a fair description of them. There weren't any finger prints or any clues whatsoever except what the woman remembered. She was sure that she

could identify the robbers though. They got
a couple of thousand dollars' worth of jewels.
This is one big story that Donald Carter didn't
get a chance to report.''

''That's good. And there may be bigger
ones.''

Judy was smiling as she hung up the receiver.
She would have stayed and talked to the chief
longer but time slips by when exciting things
are happening and it was already late for
school.

''We'll keep quiet about the jewels,'' she
promised as she prepared to leave. ''There
won't be any story in the paper.''

''That's fine,'' he said, smiling his satisfac-
tion, ''and when the owners of this jewelry
come to claim it, maybe there'll be a reward
waiting for you and your brother.''

''I don't think he would take it,'' Judy re-
plied, remembering the many rewards he had
refused after the Roulsville flood. ''The sat-
isfaction of helping you catch the robbers is
about all we want. By the way, Chief Kelly,
did they ever find out who robbed the Lees
last summer?''

Judy asked this question with palpitating heart and half expected the chief to tell her it was none of her affair.

"Not yet," he answered. "That's another piece of thievery I'm laying at the door of Vine's youngest son. You know, there's a reward up for those jewels too. Dig around a bit more and you may find them."

"You really think so!"

"Sure, and why not?" Chief Kelly produced a note pad and handed it to her. "Better put your telephone number down here. I may want to get in touch with you some time in a hurry."

CHAPTER XI

UNDER SUSPICION

Judy walked on to school deep in thought. So Vine Thompson sold things for robbers and nobody ever knew where she sold them. What an opportunity!

And Chief Kelly thought there was a chance of finding more jewels, maybe even Lorraine's ring. Judy had visions of secret panels in the wall, hidden stairways and many other mysterious means of concealment. And they hadn't even explored the attic! What possible difference could bad odors make when such thrilling adventures awaited them. The world seemed to smile for Judy as she entered the study hall, a little late for her first class.

Kay Vincent edged up to her after the period was over and whispered something that Judy couldn't quite hear.

"The jewels," she repeated. "What did you do with them?"

"I haven't any jewels," Judy replied.

"But you did have," Kay insisted. "Dickie told us. I don't believe your brother found them in a tree."

"Nobody asked you to believe it," Judy retorted. "Horace may only have been kidding. I don't think myself that jewelry is very apt to be found in trees."

She was deliberately misleading Kay because she had promised to keep their discovery of the jewels a secret.

But Harry Vincent's daughter was too shrewd to be deceived. She knew too much about Vine Thompson and her mysterious house.

At noon Judy noticed that Kay was the center of an interested group of listeners and she caught the word "jewels" as she passed them. Oh, if Horace had only had sense enough to keep still. Whatever had possessed him to talk about anything as important as that to a ten-year-old boy?

Lois was not in school again that day and Judy felt very much like an outsider as the other girls stood in circles talking. Every once in a while they would glance at her and then say something else in a whisper. Kay seemed to have gained some additional information and was passing it on with all the zest of a town crier. Lorraine was listening eagerly and every now and then Judy noticed her blonde curls bobbing in agreement with Kay. Just before the bell rang the whole crowd of girls approached Judy.

"We want to hear about the jewels," Betty and Marge insisted.

"Did your brother really find them in a tree?" Lorraine wanted to know.

"I never said he did," Judy replied vaguely.

"I told you she wouldn't talk," Kay Vincent whispered spitefully. "They probably kept the jewelry for themselves. Anyone who would live in Vine Thompson's house wouldn't have any scruples about taking stolen goods."

She had meant Judy to hear and the angry flush that spread over her face told Kay that she had added fuel to the fire of her resentment.

"If you didn't find any jewelry," Kay charged, "what was your brother talking about?"

"Curiosity killed a cat," was Judy's ungracious reply.

Judy walked away.

Kay had a temper equally as hot as Judy's own. This answer did not please her and, although she made no further comment, she felt very much vexed that a new girl should put her at a disadvantage before her friends.

"There's something more to this jewelry business than that Bolton girl has told us," she confided later to Lorraine. "If not, why did she blush when I said she probably kept some of the jewelry out for herself?"

"And she was wearing a ring," added Constance Gray, another member of this select group of high school girls.

"Was she?" exclaimed Lorraine. "I had a ring stolen last summer when a robber took mother's bracelet and pearls. Was this ring a good one?"

"I didn't notice."

"I'll find out about it," promised Kay with a vigorous nod of her head. "There's Judy now, walking with Betty. I don't admire Betty's taste."

The others agreed with this unkind statement as Kay quickened her steps to overtake Judy.

She turned around in surprise as Kay Vincent took her hand. But, without knowing why she did it, Judy pulled it away.

"I just wanted to see your ring," said Kay. "There's no harm in that, is there?"

"Curious again?" she asked with a curl of her lip. The other girls she liked in spite of all their unkindnesses but Kay Vincent she simply couldn't stand. Judy, naturally an out-spoken girl, had never learned to conceal her likes and dislikes.

"We noticed you were wearing a ring," Constance attempted to explain, "and Kay just wanted to see it."

"I see. But I have been wearing this ring all the time. Kay has had plenty of chances to look at it."

"I never noticed it before," Kay said and several of the other girls echoed, "Neither did I."

"Where did you get it?" asked Lorraine suddenly.

"What difference does it make?"

Promises she had made seemed to have tied Judy hand and foot. Chief Kelly, of course, had an excellent reason for requesting secrecy but, all at once, her pledge to Lois seemed absurd and childish. It seemed unfair to Lorraine. Still it was a pledge and Judy's sense of loyalty prevented her from breaking it.

"Well," charged Kay, "if it doesn't make any difference where you got that ring why did you blush this noon when I said you might have kept it out of that jewelry your brother found in a tree?"

"Kay Vincent, do you mean to insinuate that I stole this ring?" asked Judy, glaring at her.

"You might not call it stealing. Anyone that would live——"

"Don't say that again, Kay," coaxed Constance, pulling at her arm. "That's a little too mean. Judy's right. What difference does it make?"

"Connie Gray, do you mean to say it makes no difference if one of our classmates is a thief?"

"But Kay," protested Betty, "maybe she isn't."

"And maybe she is," put in Lorraine, her eyes resting suspiciously on the ruby ring.

Judy felt her cheeks growing hot. What right had these girls to stand there accusing her of such a dreadful thing?

"Well," insisted Kay, "if you didn't take that ring out of Vine Thompson's stolen jewelry, where did you get it?"

"At the five and ten cent store, where you get all your jewelry," was Judy's angry retort.

She walked away from the group of astonished girls, glad that she had said something as cruel as Kay's cutting remarks, glad that she hadn't told them Lois gave her the ring. They wouldn't have believed it anyway.

But Judy was to bitterly regret these hasty words of hers in the morning.

CHAPTER XII

WHO KEEPS THE RING?

IT HAPPENED just before school the next morning. Judy had called for Lois only to learn that her friend was still suffering with a cold and would not be in school that day. She walked on alone and arrived at school about twenty minutes before the first bell rang. She had time to tidy her hair in the girls' lavatory and, as she stood by the basin washing her hands, she noticed a group of girls watching her. Judy had removed her ring and placed it on the rim of the wash bowl right next to the faucets. She reached for a paper towel to dry her hands.

With the agility of a cat, Kay Vincent's hand reached out and took possession of the ring. Lorraine Lee leaned forward to see it and a surprised "Ah" went up from the group of girls.

"Just what I thought," declared Kay. "Those burglars sold their plunder to Vine

Thompson and Judy's brother found where she had hidden the jewels. Instead of reporting it to the police as they should, they decided to keep them. And to prove it, here is Lorraine's stolen ring.''

"That isn't Lorraine's ring," cried Judy. "It's mine. I've had it all the time."

"Oh, and you bought it at the five and ten cent store." Kay held the ring aloft derisively. "I ask you, girls, does this look like a ten cent ring?"

"It isn't a ten cent ring. It was a gift——"

"But you said yesterday——"

"I know," Judy interrupted tremulously. "But—but you were teasing me—and I was angry. That wasn't true. But the ring is mine, really it is. Please give it back to me."

Lorraine had taken it in her own hands.

"There!" she exclaimed. "I knew it." She pointed out the fine engraving inside the circle of gold. "See, it's Lois' initials. It's the same ring she gave me four years ago—and it was a pledge. I treasured it so. Then it was stolen and I thought I never would see it again." Lorraine's voice broke and her eyes filled with happy tears as she slipped the ring on her finger. "Oh," she sighed ecstatically, "I'm so glad it was found."

Judy's heart went out to her. Both of them were tangled in a web of circumstances that could not be explained without breaking a pledge. She could not blame Lorraine for believing the ring was hers. But, and this was the thought that cut like a knife, if Lorraine kept the ring they would all think Judy had stolen it—and lied. Oh, she could have bitten her tongue for saying that it came from the ten cent store.

The bell rang for classes and its echo buzzed in Judy's throbbing head. When Lorraine walked out of the room wearing Lois' pledge of friendship a strange feeling had taken possession of the wronged girl. She felt that Lorraine was walking away with her friendship for Lois as well as with her ring.

Just how she managed to get through that day, Judy never knew. She blundered dreadfully in her lessons and when the last bell rang for dismissal she felt glad to get away from the disapproving glances of her school mates. For once she did not mind walking home alone. She felt unequal to the task of talking with anyone. So, when she heard feet hurrying to over-take her, Judy quickened her own steps.

"Wait a minute! Where's the fire?" called a girlish voice behind her and she turned around to see Irene Lang, a little out of breath but smiling.

"Well, how's high school? Like it as well as you thought you would?" asked the small mill worker.

"Oh, it's all right," returned Judy, but her troubled gray eyes denied the truth of what she said.

"Why, what's the matter?" asked Irene, very much concerned. "Are your studies too hard or are the girls——"

"It's all right, I said," replied Judy impatiently. "How does it happen you are not at the mill? I thought you worked from seven till five."

"I do," Irene assured her, "but we had a day off today. A shipment of raw silk didn't get in on time so we couldn't work."

"Aren't you lucky?"

"Well, not exactly. You see," explained Irene, "when we don't work we don't get paid. I always dread holidays. I thought maybe we could spend this one together and get better acquainted. Would you like to?"

Judy hesitated, remembering Louis' request, but she could not find it in her heart to say anything unkind to Irene.

"What will we do?" she asked.

"Talk," replied Irene.

"But I don't want to talk. I don't feel like talking."

"Then we won't talk. We'll play games or I'll play the piano for you. Anything you like."

"How kind you are!" Judy exclaimed. "If you'd play and sing for me like you do for your father, I'd love it."

Irene's face beamed with pleasure as she led her into her own clean little house. The floors were bare except for a few rag rugs and the piano was, by far, the nicest piece of furniture in the room. Irene walked over to it and touched it lovingly.

"I couldn't have had this," she said, "if I hadn't gone to work. I bought it second hand, out of my own pay, and taught myself how to play it. I can afford to keep it tuned too—but we won't talk any more. You said you didn't want to."

"I like to listen though," replied Judy. And for the next hour there were so many beautiful things for her to hear that she began to feel better about the ring.

Irene sang some of the good old-fashioned songs that everybody loves, some more modern ones and some delightful negro spirituals. She talked too, about her ambitions to become a choir singer and the new violin she intended to buy with her next pay check. She did not mention high school again or ask Judy a single question until she was ready to leave. Then, rather timidly, she began.

"Did you—did you find out anything about the voice? Or don't you want to talk about that either?"

"You funny girl!" exclaimed Judy. "I wondered why you hadn't asked about the ghosts. I'm always willing to talk about them. Sometimes I think I need them, like I needed your music, to keep my mind off other things. But I've never heard that voice. I'd sort of like to."

And she went on until dark telling Irene about the haunted house, the crying, the rapping and the apparition in the window.

"We are solving some of these mysteries," she finished impressively, "and we mean to solve them all."

"I think you are a brave girl," declared Irene, "to live in that house and to—and to stick it out at high school. I went once, you know. I wanted a classical education too, but Girls' High School is no place for a mill worker. Those girls have to know who your great grandfather was before they'll so much as speak to you. All I ever learned there—was how to choke back tears."

"I'm learning that too."

Judy would have said more if it hadn't been for the wall of promises that seemed to hem her in on all sides. But she was glad of Irene's sympathy and pleased when she offered to walk home with her.

The vacant factory across the street and the darkness that enveloped them when Irene turned off the light made Judy think of that other night when she had watched her playing the piano.

"Who is that boarder of yours who worked for us?" she asked.

"His name is Tom Mullins. I wish we could get rid of him without being too rude," Irene confessed. "He comes and goes at all hours of the night and helps himself to food whenever he feels like it. I often wonder where he puts it all."

"Why don't you ask him to leave?" Judy asked.

"He owes too much board money. It wouldn't pay to make him mad."

"But Irene," Judy insisted. "As it is, you're feeding him for nothing."

"I know." Irene shrugged her shoulders. "That's the way it goes." They had stopped at the door of the haunted house. "Goodbye, Judy," she called.

"Goodbye, Irene, and thanks—for cheering me up."

Judy came into the house smiling. Lois, she knew, would straighten things out in the morning. This hope so cheered her that her parents noticed nothing unusual in their daughter's manner. She said very little at dinner table but Judy was often preoccupied and Dr. Bolton, as usual, was very tired. Living in a haunted house did not help his business and nearly all the work he did was with the very poor at the hospital clinic. Sometimes patients called him to their homes but the reception room which Judy had helped to arrange so tastefully was usually vacant.

That night Judy's room was so quiet that the silence irritated her almost as much as the rappings had done. Could all the noises have been caused by the tree, she wondered. She had noticed as she came in that Horace's ropes were still securely tied around the two main branches.

But Judy was in no mood for solving mysteries. Even the prospect of finding Lorraine's ring did not look bright to her and, weary both in mind and body, Judy was glad to be in bed early.

"Lois will straighten things out in the morning," was her last thought before she went to sleep.

CHAPTER XIII

EXPLORATION

"Lois will straighten things out," was the first thing that flashed across Judy's mind when she awoke in the morning. She even hummed a little tune as she dressed herself. Afterwards she ate a hearty breakfast and started early for school.

On the porch she almost collided with her father. He carried his satchel and Judy knew he had just returned from an early morning professional call.

"I've been to see a friend of yours," he announced cheerfully.

Judy's heart skipped a beat.

"Not Lois?"

"Yes, Judy girl. But don't look so frightened. She's not seriously ill. In fact it's a very light case of Scarlet Fever——"

"Scarlet Fever! Oh, Dad! Not Scarlet Fever!" cried Judy suddenly grown panicky with the thought that Lois would be out of school for a month or more.

Dr. Bolton turned to Judy in alarm.

"My dear girl! What is it?" He led her back into the house and pulled her onto his knee. "Come, tell your old Dad all about it."

Between sobs, Judy related the whole story and when she had finished the doctor patted her shoulder.

"Well, well," he sympathized. "It looks as if we were into a hornet's nest. But I'll talk to Lois tomorrow and see what can be done about returning the ring. Of course the house is in quarantine and that makes it bad. And this other affair about the jewels—well, Judy girl, I can trust to your head to work out a good solution."

In the dark days that followed Judy learned just how much sympathy can do to ease heartache. Mrs. Bolton was always doing little unexpected things for her, such as buying new clothes or trinkets for her room. Horace was all contrition and blamed himself a dozen times a day for being the cause of Judy's trouble.

"Next time I'll know enough to keep my mouth shut," he said regretfully. "As if that big robbery story wasn't enough to talk about. The police are almost sure from the woman's description of the burglars that one of them was Vine Thompson's son.''

"He probably was," Judy replied with a surprising lack of enthusiasm.

Even the factory girls got wind of the trouble Judy was having at school and braved the perils of the haunted house to offer their sympathy.

"Those snobs are just scheming things, tryin' to kick you out of high school," declared Sally Belaski. "They think it's some fancy boardin' school fit for only rich folks, that's what they think."

"And that pretty little hussy of a Lorraine Lee would be the first one to do a thing like that," added Ada.

"She's not to blame," Judy defended loyally. "It's just the way things happened. She has plenty of reason to believe the ring is really hers."

"She's probably jealous of you and Lois." This was Irene's explanation. "Jealousy does terrible things sometimes," she went on. "Judy, why don't you give it up? Things 'ike that don't happen at Industrial High."

"That's right," agreed Sally. "I'd give it up too if I were you."

"Dad," said Judy, turning to the long figure who lay on the sofa, tired after a strenuous day at the hospital clinic. "When do you think a person ought to give up?"

"In my business," he replied, "we never give up until the patient is dead. Your patient isn't dead, Judy girl. She's only got Scarlet Fever. She felt very sorry about your troubles when I told her and promised me that as soon as she could she would explain things to Lorraine."

Another staunch friend who came to sympathize was Peter Dobbs. He blamed all the trouble on promises.

"If I had my way," he declared vigorously. "There wouldn't be any such things as pledges of secrecy. Everything would be out and out facts. Sometimes I think it must have been some ridiculous promise that keeps Grandma and Granddad from telling me who I am."

"It could be," Judy agreed. "At least they must have promised each other not to tell. I know how you feel about it, Peter. I wish I could help."

"Oh, that's nothing compared to what you're up against." He dismissed his own troubles with a gesture of his hand. "Nobody suspects me of stealing, or having anything to do with stolen goods. Gosh! It must be terrible. And the deuce of it is that Lois is in quarantine and can't even write to Lorraine. When she is strong enough to telephone——"

"Oh, I hadn't thought of that," Judy broke in excitedly and then her face fell. "Even if Lorraine does know the ring is mine, Peter, it won't make her any more friendly. I think Irene Lang is right and she is a little bit jealous. To know that Lois has pledged her friendship to me won't help matters one bit."

"It's a Chinese puzzle all right," Peter agreed soberly. He had called for the express purpose of cheering up Judy and setting her mind to work on mysteries again. Frankly, he was curious.

"Why don't you forget about this confounded ring and get busy scaring up ghosts?" he asked. "Here Halloween is not three weeks off and you haven't begun making plans for that party."

"But Peter," objected Judy gloomily. "There can't be any party now. Who would come?"

"I would, for one," he answered, "and so would Grandma and Granddad. You have no reason to think that Arthur and Lois wouldn't come, have you?"

"Would Lois be over having Scarlet Fever by then?"

"Sure, she ought to be back to school a week before Halloween."

It seemed a long time to Judy. "Well," she said, "let's wait then. I haven't the heart to go planning parties now."

"That doesn't sound like you, Judy, where's all that old-fashioned courage you used to have?"

"I still have it, Peter. And how I need it! All right I'll plan the party. I—I'm not going to be a quitter. Only Peter, the ghosts have gone back on us too. We haven't seen or heard an unnatural thing for a week. I've been listening and listening for that voice that folks say they've heard but I never hear a thing."

"That's too bad," he sympathized. "We could create quite a sensation if we solved the mystery of the voice. Horace told me about the jewels you found——"

"He found them. I didn't," Judy interrupted.

"Yes, I know, and it's supposed to be a secret but, as a close friend of the family, I have been told. By the way, did you ever get your reward?"

"Not yet, but Horace has agreed to accept it if I will take half. He has the strangest way of figuring things. Says that if I hadn't heard the rappings he wouldn't have climbed the tree and found the jewels."

"Aha, I see," laughed Peter, "so he figures that you helped find them—and he's quite right. It's like the flood and your part in that. Horace has his little sister to thank for a lot of things."

"Indeed I do," spoke a voice from the doorway and there stood Horace, his hands still dirty from type at the newspaper office.

"And the dickens of it all is," he continued, "here Judy is in a fix and we can't do a thing to help her out. It makes me boil. I tried to talk to the boss about it today. You know, Peter. Lorraine's father is the man I work for.

but he says school girls are bound to have their troubles and the best thing for their men folks to do, is to let them fight it out. A pretty one-sided fight, I call it.''

"No," declared Judy bravely. "I have the right on my side. So let's forget it until Lois comes back to school. I've promised Peter to keep right on planning the party so let's get busy investigating those noises that used to bother us. Now that Peter's here, Horace, why can't we explore that attic?''

"Capital!" exclaimed Peter Dobbs. "I am honored to be a member of such a brave expedition.''

"And I'll get the boxes," promised Horace as he hurried after them.

Together they trooped up the stairs and into Judy's room where the boxes were, once more, stacked nearly to the ceiling.

"Who'll be first?" asked Horace.

"Well," laughed Judy, growing enthusiastic in spite of herself, "I might as well warn you, there's a most awful smell up there. Some one with a good nose ought to go first.''

"That's me," grinned Peter, pointing to the object in question. "There isn't much of it, but what there is can stand bad smells. My great grandfather was a garbage collector."

This remark caused more merriment for Judy and her brother both realized that Peter's great grandfather really might have been exactly that for all he knew.

"Here goes," cried Peter. "You two hold on there. A hundred and fifty pounds is going up."

"Yes," chuckled Horace as he gripped the packing boxes, "and almost six feet of them at that."

Then the big form of Peter Dobbs disappeared through the opening in the ceiling.

"The air up here isn't exactly laden with perfume," the two below heard his muffled call. "Ah, I have it. Prepare yourselves for the worst. Here's a box of old rags with an unholy odor to it and here, oh good grief, are the decayed remains of many an uneaten meal."

"Let's have them," shouted Horace. "Throw them down and I'll catch. Smell any more rats?"

"No, but you can't catch these. Clear a space and I'll throw them down and hope to heaven they land right side up."

"O. K."

Judy and Horace stepped to one side as the two boxes crashed down from the ceiling. As soon as the space was cleared, Peter jumped down after them and the three young people started outside to make a bonfire of the boxes, contents and all.

"I wonder," mused Peter, "what all that food was for. Looks as if something was supposed to eat it. In fact, it looks as if something *had* eaten some of it."

"The ghost, of course," said Horace seriously.

After the refuse had gone up in smoke and the young people had thoroughly washed themselves, they again ascended the stairs to continue their explorations.

"Do you suppose," asked Judy, "that the bad smell is completely gone?"

"Hardly," answered Peter as he began repiling the boxes which served as a ladder. "Odors linger for a long time in a closed place like that. I don't suppose those round windows are built to open."

"Oh, yes," replied Horace. "They're

screened, that's all. Plenty of air comes in through the screens.''

"I have heard," ventured Judy, "of destroying bad odor by burning papers or rags. Couldn't we try that?"

"And set the house on fire!" exclaimed Horace.

"No, burn them in an old pail. I'll go get one now."

When she returned Peter and Horace were up in the attic again. She scrambled up after them and exhibited a battered tin bucket that she had found in the cellar.

"But you didn't bring any papers to burn," protested Horace.

"It looks to me as if there were plenty of papers up here already," she replied. "Why not burn them?"

"That's so," agreed Peter as he began collecting them and stuffing them into the pail. Judy had also brought a flashlight and she held it closer.

"Wait a minute," she exclaimed. "Hadn't we better see what we're burning first? What's this?"

CHAPTER XIV

DISCOVERY

JUDY exhibited a pack of letters, mouse-eaten around the edges, yellowed with age and tied with a faded blue ribbon.

"I declare," ejaculated Peter as he opened one and saw the words, "My dearest Big Boy," "if it doesn't look like somebody's love letters. Let's save them and read them later."

"That's what I say," assented Horace, "and I make the motion that we burn no more of anything until we have examined it carefully. The idea! Burning letters when we have so many mysteries to solve!"

"I've always wanted to read somebody's love letters," mused Judy.

Peter grinned good-naturedly as he stuffed the pack in his pockets for future perusal. "Some day you'll be reading your own, I hope."

"Nonsense!" she exclaimed. "If I don't

get a look at these it's probably my last chance. Hurry, Peter, and light those old newspapers. There must be enough in the pail by now. I'm anxious to open that big trunk. Look, it has tags from Chicago and San Francisco on it."

"Yes, old Vine did a good bit of traveling too," said Peter as he struck a match and touched it to the papers that were stuffed in the bottom of the pail. Instantly the flames shot almost to the roof.

"Help!" cried Horace. "Somebody's used this pail for kerosene. Quick! Let's get out of here before we're burned alive."

Instead of scrambling for the opening, however, Judy darted in the other direction and caught hold of an old coat that had been flung across the trunk. This she crammed into the flaming pail while Peter stamped out a few sparks that were beginning to kindle on the rough floor boards. Horace, not to be outdone by the others, grabbed his cap which he had worn as a protection against dust and cobwebs and whipped out another spark that had caught in the rafters.

"Well," said Judy after things were a bit more quiet and the air decidedly purer from the effect of burning things, "we put it out, didn't we?"

"*You* put it out, you mean," corrected Horace. "Peter and I were ready to run and let the thing burn."

"I saved the trunk anyway," she laughed. "Now let's see what's in it. If only it isn't locked."

The trunk was a long affair of the wardrobe variety, nearly new and in good condition. The brass locks on either end most certainly could not be opened without a key.

"What a shame!" cried Judy, "but anyway we can take it down to my room and keep it there. With all those tags people will think I am somebody who travels."

"Some traveler, you!" teased Peter. "Thirty miles from Dry Brook Hollow to Farringdon!"

Moving the trunk from the attic to Judy's room did not prove to be such an easy matter as it had seemed. They were obliged to call Dr. Bolton to help, which he did good-naturedly. Judy and Horace heaved it down through the opening while Peter and the doctor, who were stronger, caught hold of it and lowered it to the floor. It made a good window seat once it was in position and Judy promptly dusted it and placed some cushions on it. The Ghost, who had been sleeping on Blackberry's cushion, seeing a new place to nap, stretched himself lazily and hopped up onto the trunk.

"Didn't know you had a new kitten," remarked Peter, eyeing the white cat curiously, "or did Blackberry fall into a bottle of peroxide?"

Just then Blackberry himself came into the room, sniffed his own cushion, took three turns and lay down while Peter looked on bewildered.

"That white cat is Horace's idea of a surprise," Judy explained. "But I surprised him and gave him right back again. If you think he's thin now you should have seen him the day he was given to me. Just skin and bones, really. But Horace has been a good master to him. Treats him better than I do Blackberry. He even buys catnip for him."

"Quite a contrast to the other cat," Peter observed. "What do you call him?"

"The Ghost."

Peter gave a start. "Good Heavens, as if there weren't ghosts enough in the house. Whose idea was that?"

Horace grinned sheepishly and confessed. "I'm beginning to get quite a kick out of this haunted house business," he continued. "And I must say that party Judy is planning is going to be a wow. Come on, let's finish exploring the attic before it gets too dark."

They climbed up and searched around for another half hour, discovering a few more letters, some books which looked like good reading and some more magazines. Then Horace stumbled over something and turned around in horror.

"A gun!" he exclaimed as he stood staring at it.

"And I'll bet it's loaded too," cried Peter. "It would be like Vine Thompson to keep a loaded gun on hand. Lucky thing she didn't have it handy when the cops raided this place. Here, Judy, don't touch it. I'll carry it downstairs. I've been on hunting trips and know how to handle it."

"You're welcome," she laughed. "I wonder what else we'll find. Horace, do you suppose you could walk over those beams without falling through the plaster, and get that bird cage?"

"Over by the round window? Sure." And he began walking cautiously along the beam.

Peter Dobbs had gone downstairs with the gun and had just returned. He called up from the room below.

"Most finished up there?"

"Coming down in just a minute," Horace called back. "Guess you'd better save yourself the trouble of climbing up again. Go on down, Judy, like a good girl, and keep Peter company."

"Aren't you going to let me take the cage?" she asked as he lifted it from its dusty resting place.

"No, never mind. I'll take care of that."

Judy left the attic reluctantly, wondering why Horace had suddenly decided to quit exploring. She asked Peter if he knew why but the Dobbs boy declared he hadn't the slightest idea.

"Wonder why he doesn't come down now— with that bird cage," said Judy after about five minutes of waiting.

"Climb up again and see," suggested Peter.

Judy did so quietly and Horace did not look up when she poked her head through the open ing. There he sat cross-legged beside the lighted lantern, writing things in his black notebook. Sprawled on his knee was something that looked to Judy like the wings of a dead bat. She wondered that Horace could be so intensely interested in such a gruesome object. Suddenly he burst out laughing, all by himself, without realizing that his sister was watching. She descended cautiously so that he would not hear.

"Well," began Peter when she was safely down again. Then he stopped and stared at her. "What's the matter? You look as if you had seen a ghost."

Judy laughed nervously. "Come on, Peter," she coaxed, "let's go downstairs and leave Horace alone. He's interested in some dead thing up there, so interested that he didn't even know I saw him."

"You don't say! Was it something little?" he asked.

"Quite little, looked like a bat."

Peter whistled his surprise. "Too bad it's so late or I could stay and help you unsnarl the latest mystery." Then he grabbed Judy's hand and said, half in earnest, "Say, young lady, maybe it's a dead ghost. You haven't heard any lately."

"I shouldn't wonder," she replied. "Can you come up tomorrow night so we can look over those letters again? That is, if Horace doesn't get hold of them. He seems to have an eye on all the mysterious things. Maybe you'd better keep them, Peter, but promise me you won't read them."

"On my honor," he promised. "I know you're curious. And say, I've got a bunch of keys at home, all sizes. Maybe one of them will fit that trunk."

"Oh, I do hope so," cried Judy. "Don't forget now. Be here about seven o'clock. Now I'll go up and rout Horace out of the attic so I can do a little studying before I go to bed."

"Need any help?" asked Peter.

"What? Studying?"

"No. Routing out Horace."

"Think not. I'll call you if I do. Look!" she exclaimed, "all the neighbors in the row are out watching his shadowy form through the round attic windows. They'll be telling ghost stories till midnight."

"What fun!" cried Peter.

"And haven't we had a glorious time," en-thused Judy. "That trunk! Those letters! And whatever it is that Horace has found! Goodness, I feel all shivery with guessing about it. Horace has such a lot of secrets."

"So I suspected," laughed Peter as he bade the bright-eyed girl goodnight.

"Don't forget, tomorrow night at seven, with the keys!" she called as he swung his long body down the steps to the street.

CHAPTER XV

IT SEEMED almost as if Judy lived in two separate worlds, the day time world at school where she recited her lessons mechanically, avoiding the accusing eyes of her classmates and the world of adventure in the evening. She was pondering on this unusual state of affairs when, at five minutes of seven, a rap sounded at the door. Thinking it was Peter, she ran to answer it. Instead of the Dobbs boy, however, Irene Lang stood in the doorway.

Judy was so frankly taken aback that Irene asked, "What's the matter? Aren't you glad I came?"

"Of course I'm glad," she replied. "You're always welcome, Irene."

"I just wanted to show you my new violin." She held it up proudly. "Isn't it a peach?"

Although Judy knew very little about music and less about musical instruments she admired the violin to please Irene.

"Can you play it?" she asked.

"Oh, yes, I learned on Kitty Dugan's. She's the forelady at the mill and a perfect darling."

"Does she live down town?"

Irene seemed surprised. "Of course not. None of the mill girls live down town. The down town girls, if they work at all, work in stores or offices."

"I can't see why working in a store is any better than working at the mill," observed Judy.

"I can't either," declared Irene. "I really think the mill girls have more fun. We all have pretty big ambitions too. A lot of us come in to work from Industrial High and we all like each other."

"I wish I could say just half those nice things about the crowd at Girls' High," sighed Judy. "You were right, Irene, about learning to choke back tears. I'm learning, all right. Sometimes I think if we didn't have such good times in the evening I simply couldn't bear it."

"You poor kid!"

Judy smiled wanly. "I almost did forget it yesterday," she went on. "For all of two hours I didn't think of it once. Peter Dobbs was here and he's coming again tonight. Come, Irene, let's hear that new violin of yours while we're waiting."

"Are you sure you want me here?"

That was just it. Judy wasn't sure but she was trying her best to treat Irene kindly. "Of course I want you here," she said. "Will you play for me?"

Irene complied with this request gladly but she had no more than seated herself on the lounge and touched the strings when Peter's rap sounded on the door. She stopped playing abruptly and opened her blue eyes wide. Judy and Peter were having a most unusual conversation and she could not help hearing.

"Hello, Peter! What's the matter? You look scared."

"Who wouldn't be scared," he answered. "Judy, I saw that ghost in the attic window again."

"Really, Peter? I didn't think that ghost was there any more."

"But I tell you I saw him. And I heard the voice! It called out 'hello stranger' just like Donald Carter said. And I looked up at the attic window and there was that ghost—talking.

The voice came right from the window and the ghost was there!''

"But Peter, there wasn't anything unnatural when we climbed up yesterday—except——"

"That dead thing Horace found!" exclaimed Peter Dobbs. "Where is he now?"

"Said he had a date with a ghost," Judy answered, "but I thought he was only joking. Do you suppose he heard the voice? Did he act scared?"

"Not scared, but awful mysterious and funny. Then he disappeared and I haven't seen him for an hour or more."

"Could he be up in the attic now?" Peter asked this question in a hoarse whisper.

"No. He went outside. I think that dead thing must have been a dead bat."

"Oh!" gasped Irene. She had heard of vampires—ghosts that took the form of bats and was actually terrified.

Peter turned suddenly on his heel. "Why the deuce didn't you tell me you had company?" he asked.

"I forgot. Gee, Peter, how could I remember anything? You had me all goose-flesh for a minute."

"Me too," chimed in Irene. "Judy, could anything—could anything have happened to Horace?"

"Why?"

"I couldn't help hearing what you said," she confessed. "Maybe I'm superstitious and silly but sometimes bats do—bats are—something more than just bats."

Judy laughed nervously. "We're all acting silly. We weren't going to get scared, you know. We were going to have some fun with the ghosts."

"You can't have fun with dead things," objected Peter.

"Horace seems to have fun with—with that bat, or whatever it was."

"Maybe it wasn't dead," Irene whispered.

Suddenly Judy realized that this little mill girl was hearing more than she ought to hear. She hadn't intended to let Irene in on the mysteries but now it was too late.

"What about the keys?" she asked Peter. "Did you bring them? Oh, goody!" He jingled them in his pocket. "And the letters?"

Peter produced them. "Well, which shall it be first—reading the love letters, opening old

Vine's trunk or finding out what's in the attic?''

''I don't want to go up in the attic now,'' she demurred. ''Irene, suppose you play us a tune first. Peter and I need something to quiet our nerves.''

''I know a piece called 'The Dance of the Ghosts,' '' ventured Irene. ''Would that be all right?''

''Quite appropriate,'' declared Peter. ''Let's hear it.''

The lights in the room were dim. Irene drew the bow across the strings of her violin, and it seemed as if shadowy forms were gliding across the room in time to the weird melody. What it is that music can do to people, nobody knows, but whatever it is, ''The Dance of the Ghosts'' did it to Judy and Peter—simply carried them away to a world of lights and shadows where ghostly things are also beautiful. The tune died away into silence, but for a moment no one spoke. Then Judy said the only thing she could think of to say.

''Irene, you're wonderful!''

''I quite agree with you,'' said Peter Dobbs. ''Whoever taught you to play like that?''

"She taught herself," answered Judy quickly, "and that makes her all the more wonderful."

"I should say so," agreed Peter. "She's just the finishing touch that you need to make your ghost party a success."

Irene looked puzzled. Judy hesitated. She had never told any of the mill girls about the party because she had planned to invite only members of her class at Girls' High School or boys who, like Peter and Arthur, were part of the down-town crowd. Then an idea occurred to her that seemed to solve the problem.

"We're all going to come to the party masked," she said. "No one is to guess who the others are. It's a Halloween Party that I'm having and the object of it is to explain all the mysteries of this house. If we solve the talking ghost mystery and get this ring business cleared up at school, it ought to be a whopping big party. Would you like to come, Irene, and bring your violin? Would you play that 'Dance of the Ghosts' as part of our entertainment?"

"Would I like to? Why, I'd love to," cried Irene. "Judy, how good you are to invite me."

"You're not invited yet," laughed Judy, "only asked. You'll get your invitation later. You too, Peter, and your grandparents."

"And say," he put in, "why couldn't we read these love letters at the ghost party? They're pretty sure to be exciting."

"And maybe the trunk will be full of costumes for us to wear." Judy was hopping all around the room in her excitement.

"Come on, girls, let's see if these keys fit," called Peter as he started up the stairs. In Judy's room, he stopped short and the girls who had followed him, stopped too. A curious scraping sound issued from the ceiling. It sounded like something rising from a sitting posture and walking cautiously across the beams. Then something rattled and the scraping sound was heard again.

"Sounds like somebody was up there," whispered Judy.

"Maybe Horace." Peter cupped his hands and shouted up to the ceiling. "Hey there! Give the ghosts a rest and let's get at this treasure trunk."

No answer, except the scraping sound again

and the grating of what sounded like a cover sliding onto a box.

"Ugh!" shivered Irene. "It might be the lid sliding onto a coffin."

Peter looked scared too and Judy looked puzzled. Neither of them had any inclination, just at that moment, to pile up the boxes and investigate as they had done the night before.

Then all three of them heard it, a harsh throaty call that echoed weirdly down from the ceiling.

"Hello-o-o Stra-a-a-anger!"

They stood for a moment absolutely silent. The unbelievable had happened. They had heard the voice!

"Peter," Judy whispered at last, "do me a favor, will you?"

"Anything," the Dobbs boy replied.

"Well then, don't tell Horace that we heard it. He's busy solving all the mysteries and I want to solve this one myself. After all, it's my party."

"All right," promised Peter. "We won't let on, will we, Irene?"

The mill girl, still frightened, promised in a

weak voice just as Horace bounded up the steps, three at a time.

"Who's been up my tree?" he shouted.

"Your tree?" questioned Judy in a puzzled voice. "I didn't know you had a tree."

"The tree out in front. Somebody's taken the ropes." He stopped short. "Hang it all!" he exclaimed. "I'll be giving everything away before the party if I'm not careful. What have you people been doing? Investigating?"

"Not yet," Judy replied. "Irene was playing her violin for us and Peter brought some keys."

"Fine, but let's tackle that attic first," Horace suggested. He did not seem at all afraid. It was incredible.

"Would you *dare* go up?" asked Irene.

"Sure I would," and he began piling up the boxes. "Who wants to come with me?"

"I will," volunteered Judy. Her curiosity had been aroused.

Irene held back. This was a little too much for the somewhat superstitious mill girl who had heard of vampires in the form of bats. So Peter stayed downstairs to keep her company.

Horace shoved the lid off the queer little door

and he and his sister crawled inside. Everything looked exactly as it had looked the day before.

"Are you sure you saw something up there?" Horace quizzed his sister after they had let themselves down from the ceiling and stood in Judy's room again.

"I'm not sure of anything any more," she answered. "But you act pretty sure of yourself. Just what *have* you found out, Horace Bolton?"

"At the ghost party," he replied, "everything will be divulged and expounded."

"The voice too?" questioned Peter.

"Everything."

"Oh," cried Judy. Disappointment sounded in her voice. "You've solved all the mysteries —all of them?"

"Aren't you glad?" Horace asked in surprise. "Now you can have your party."

No answer. Judy was kneeling before the trunk and examining the lock. Peter handed her the keys and while she tried them, one by one, the others all knelt beside her and watched eagerly.

Some of the keys would not go into the brass

locks at all; some of them slid almost through and still others stuck and had to be pulled out by force. But not one key in the bunch would turn so much as a sixteenth of an inch.

"What are we going to do now?" asked Peter after the last key had been tried.

"Break it with an axe," was Horace's suggestion.

"And spoil that beautiful trunk!" exclaimed Irene.

"No you don't," cried Judy. "I want to use that when I go traveling."

"You forget," reproved her brother, "that we may have to turn the trunk over to the police department too. If it contains anything valuable we will."

"Then let's forget it until another key turns up somewhere. When are we going to start reading those love letters?"

"What'll we do," asked Horace, "each take some to read by himself or some one read them all aloud?"

Irene thought it would be more fun to have them read aloud.

"Very good," said Peter as he removed them from his pocket, "suppose you begin."

CHAPTER XVI

OLD LOVE LETTERS

AFTER Peter had drawn up a comfortable chair for Irene, the other three seated themselves on the trunk that they had been trying for half an hour to open. Irene took the first letter and examined it closely.

"It's directed to Mr. James Thompson, this address," she said.

"That's one of Vine's three sons, the youngest, I believe." Peter had learned a good deal about the Thompson family history by making inquiries among his friends.

"Well, somebody seems to have loved him in spite of his being a robber," remarked Irene with a smile. "And what a nice handwriting—but the ink is so faded." She sniffed the envelope. "It smells like lavender. The girl must have been a fastidious creature."

"I'd rather hear the letter than smell it," said Peter Dobbs dryly.

141

"So would I! So would I!" echoed the others.

"Very well, then. Here it is," and she began to read.

" 'Dearest Jimmie Boy: At last I am alone and can steal time to write to you. Here's a thousand kisses before some one interrupts me.

" 'Dearest, did you wait for me long? I am sorry I could not come. I can't think what has happened to Mother and Father. They never acted like this before. Father locked me in my room and I cried until I was nearly sick. He says the awfullest things about your people but I won't listen. I love you. Oh, I could say it a million times.

" 'I'll manage to meet you some way on Friday night, even if I have to jump out of the window. I wish I had long hair like the princess in my old fairy tale book. Then you could climb up on my braids. O, I'm silly, but we don't get a chance to talk. I must write so you will know how much I care. Mother says sixteen is too young to be in love, but you and I know differently. Don't we, dear?

" 'Please don't bring the ring. I couldn't wear it. We will just have to keep our engagement secret until——'

"Oh dear," sighed Irene, "the rest of the letter is gone."

"Is it?" Disappointment showed in all their faces.

"And it was so thrilling," mourned Judy.

"Cheer up," soothed Horace. "There are others like it. Let's hear the next one, Irene."

It was a Christmas card directed to James Thompson at an address in Chicago. The card showed a picture of Christmas bells and a church with sparkling tinsel snow on the roof and steeple. The sentiment underneath was this:

"All the chiming Christmas bells speak but of Love and You."

It was signed, "Your Grace."

"So Grace was the lady's name," remarked Peter.

"She wasn't a lady," said Irene reflectively. "She was just a girl, no older than I am. I think sixteen is too young to be in love, too. Suppose we change places and you read them for a while, Judy."

"I'd love to."

She took up the next envelope and found that the corner had been eaten off both the envelope and the letter inside.

"The mice must have had a *lovely* feast," joked Peter.

"Yes," agreed Judy. "This letter is even more sentimental than the other one. You'll have to help me piece it together, I guess."

They read through a lot more sweet nothings before they came to anything really important. Then this:

" 'I'll have my trunk packed and leave it at the station and then I'll come myself just before train time. Count on me this time, dearest. Mother doesn't know you are in town and neither does Father so they won't suspect a thing.

" 'Isn't it dreadful having to sneak away from home like this? And I do love Mother and Father so much—but not as much as I love you.

" 'Precious, I can't wait. Only three more days until I'll be

" 'Your loving wife,
" 'Grace.' "

"I wonder if she did marry him," mused Irene.

"The next letter will tell," observed Peter, and Judy continued reading.

" 'Little Gracie girl:' Oh, this letter is from him!"

They all leaned forward eagerly.

" 'Let Papa and Mamma see this one and who cares? It's like the song that goes

Now we are married and you may tell Pa,
For he can't help it, can he, Ma-Ma?

" 'I've found a little place for us in New York. It is not as nice as I would like it to be for my bride but it's a long way from home and mother. Our little home will be a paradise for two—with no in-laws, not even yours. I am enclosing a check. Buy yourself some finery and join me as soon as you can. Your Jim.' "

"Is her whole name on the envelope?" asked Horace.

"No, all I can see is 'Miss Grace L' or maybe it's a D or a W. Anyway, some letter with a curleyque on the front of it, and 'Ro . . .' That must be the first part of her address. Rochester—or maybe Roulsville. The letter is dated the fifth of April about twenty years ago. And it looks as if it had never been mailed."

"So I suppose we'll never know who Grace was," sighed Irene.

"Who knows?" said Judy hopefully. "There are plenty of letters left, even if they are married. Peter, wouldn't you like to read them for a little while?"

He found the task still harder for the mice had nibbled more at the bottom of the pack, but from what he could decipher Grace's letters had lost a good deal of their girlish sentiment.

"Listen to this!" he cried.

" 'Where are you? Why don't you write? I always have to send these to your mother and trust she forwards them. I can't go on like this. We're all out of money and you promised to send some.

" 'I live in the hope that you will come back to me. Oh, Jimmie, we were so happy! Your son is such a darling and now you are almost a stranger to him. The baby is better again. . . .' and the rest is torn away or eaten."

"Sounds as if Vine Thompson's sons were every bit as cruel as they were crooked," remarked Horace. "But I do feel sorry for the little woman. Let's hear what happened to her."

"You read it," Peter insisted. "Everybody else has had a turn and this is the last letter. There's a telegram underneath it but let's let that wait until last. We want to get the story as it comes."

Horace began and read the last letter through except for a few places where the mice had eaten.

" 'Jimmie, you must send me money enough to take the baby home before she dies. I can't be proud any longer, but I will not beg money of my parents.

" 'It is a disgrace the way we are living. Mrs. Vincenzo has moved us from the first floor to the darkest and dirtiest room in her house and promises to put us out in the street if the rent isn't paid by Saturday. But I don't want money to pay the rent—just enough to take these poor children home to Mother. They are both sick because the room is freezing cold. I am suffering too but the baby suffers more. She can hardly breathe.

" 'I know you don't care about us, or you would have written but you can't be hard hearted enough to let your family die. I don't care about myself. I haven't eaten for four days. Petey boy snatches what he can from the dirty Vincenzo children, but baby G . . .'

"Mice again!" exclaimed Horace. "Can't tell what the baby's name was."

"G," repeated Judy, "probably Grace after her mother."

"Well, she didn't name the boy after his father—and no wonder," remarked Horace as he resumed his reading.

" ' . . . heartache to see the children's thin little faces. This is the last time I shall write to you, Jimmie. It is your last chance to be a man. The next time, if I can find another postage stamp, I shall write to Mother and trust that she has forgiven me. How good it will seem to be at home again after this four years of misery as your wife. Grace.

" 'P. S. I am too weak to go downstairs with this letter. I tried to walk just now and almost fainted. I guess Heaven is the only home I'll ever get to. Your money may come too late for the baby too, but tell Mother about the boy.' "

"And now the telegram!" continued Horace with a tragic expression on his face. "What! It's from Mrs. Vincenzo, the Italian woman she roomed with.

" 'MORGUE HAS WIFES BODY STOP BABY DYING STOP GAVE BOY TO ORPHANAGE.' "

"And she didn't get home to her mother after all!" exclaimed Irene. "How perfectly dreadful."

"And I thought I was unhappy at school," reflected Judy. "But I guess none of us know what real trouble is. Poor Grace!"

Both the girls' eyes were bright, this time not with excitement, but with tears of sympathy for the unfortunate Grace whose girlish romance had ended so tragically. They all agreed that the letters were too sad to read at a party.

"Even the first ones," said Peter, "though they seemed silly when we started them."

Judy was still pondering upon these letters as she sat on the trunk after the others had left. She read and reread them, trying to find something that might identify Grace. Later she just sat thinking, absently fussing with her hair and manicuring her nails in preparation for school in the morning. What prompted her to pick at the lock of the trunk with the end of her nail file she did not know. She certainly had no thought that she might open it.

The nail file clicked into the small key hole and fitted as if it belonged there. Judy turned the file, first in one lock and then in the other. The trunk clicked open and, with a pounding heart, she lifted back the lid and looked inside.

CHAPTER XVII

INSIDE THE TRUNK

WHAT Judy saw would have delighted any other girl. All neatly arranged on hangers along the side of the trunk were dresses, suits and coats fit for a princess. A black evening dress with silver spangles on it was on the outside. Then, in the drawers were pale pink silk underwear and lacy edged handkerchiefs, packed in beside serviceable slip-on sweaters and sport skirts. A soft white angora tam just fitted Judy's head and reminded her of a dandelion gone to seed. Finally, she uncovered a gray tweed riding habit.

But Judy had not been looking for clothes. She had plenty. She had been searching for lost jewels and to find nothing but clothes was a disappointment. Of course the clothes were pretty. The evening dress especially would be nice to wear at her party, fixed up, of course as a masquerade costume.

Horace, in the next room, could hear his sister rummaging about while he was trying to sleep.

"Judy!" he called. "Don't you ever go to bed?"

"I am in bed," she called back. "This noise you hear is me dreaming."

"Silly child! Can't you be quiet?"

"Horace," she commanded. "Dress yourself and come in here. Then you will see for yourself why I can't be quiet."

In less than three minutes he stood in the doorway.

"Heavens and earth!" he exclaimed. "How did you open it?"

She held up the nail file. "With this," she laughed, "but you, you conscientious mortal, you'll be wanting to take it all down to the police station in the morning."

"I could hardly carry the trunk there on my back," he protested, "but, of course, we will have to notify the police."

"Let me report it," she begged. "Horace, you always take all the glory and I get the left-overs. But this trunk mystery is all mine."

"Not much of a mystery—clothes. You're

welcome,'' said Horace as he closed the **door** and went back to his own room.

Judy felt a little angry at him. He had been acting so important lately. Perhaps this being a hero had gone to his head. She would just see what was in the trunk. How she longed for a chance to surprise him.

Throwing all the clothes on her bed, Judy dove clear to the bottom of the trunk. Nothing was there, nothing at all except the clothes. She looked in all the pockets and all she found was two handkedchiefs, neither one with an initial, and a faded photograph. It was of a young man with squinted eyes and Judy guessed it was one of Vine Thompson's sons.

The handkerchiefs and the photograph were consigned to the special drawer in her dresser which she had reserved for clues. They were placed beside the mismated gloves, the green button and the thimble. Not much for a detective to work on, but at least Judy had something on Horace.

The next morning she went alone to the police station and arrived just as the old chief had finished his morning coffee. A roll lay beside the cup on his desk.

"Don't you go home at night?" Judy asked.
The chief shook his head.

"Not last night," he replied. "What now?
Found any more jewels?"

Judy smiled. The chief looked tired and it
seemed a shame to bother him with nothing
but a trunk full of old clothes.

"No jewels this time," she replied. "It's
nothing but a trunk full of clothes."

"A trunk in the tree!" exclaimed the chief.
"It must be a whopper of a tree."

"Oh no! It was in our attic."

Chief Kelly seemed interested.

"You say you found a trunk in your attic?
By the way, that gun the Dobbs boy brought in
was loaded, sure enough. Lucky thing you had
no accidents with it. Tell me, where'd you
find that?"

"In the attic too."

"Find anything else?"

"Oh, a few things," Judy replied. "I'm
having a Halloween party and we saved some
of them to, well, to demonstrate. You see, my
brother thinks he has found out what that voice
is. You have heard about it, of course?"

"Old Vine's voice? Sure. Heard it myself.

I must confess it had me stumped. When's this party of yours coming off?"

"On Halloween. It's going to be a wonderful party," Judy went on. "We've been planning it for weeks. There is going to be a regular program of entertainment, including the explanation of all the strange happenings in our house."

"All young folks coming?"

Judy laughed. Now she understood why the chief was interested.

"There will be old folks and young folks too," she told him. "Mr. and Mrs. Dobbs are coming and, of course, my father and mother will be there. Want to come?"

The chief chuckled. "Sure. Maybe you'll need me. Now, young lady, what else did you find?"

"Nothing, at least, nothing of importance to you but Horace and I figured it out that you must have skipped the attic when you raided Vine Thompson's place and so she hid some of her valuables there. If she didn't, how else would they get there?"

"That's just what I'm wondering," the chief admitted. "And so you thought we skipped the attic when we raided the place? Why, that attic was as empty as this coffee cup." He drained it and held it upside down. "Now, young lady, you're clever, figure it out for yourself."

"Thanks, Chief, I will," she promised as she started for home.

She could hardly wait to get at the trunk again. Certainly, if someone had taken the trouble to conceal it in an empty house, it must contain something more valuable than clothes. Perhaps it contained jewels.

Judy remembered that the trunk had looked large from the outside and had seemed smaller once she opened it. She also remembered that it had been very heavy. The few clothes she had found in it would not weigh much and so she came to the conclusion that the trunk could not be entirely empty.

As soon as Judy came inside the house she searched among her school things and found a ruler. Then she measured the trunk carefully from the top to the bottom on the outside. Opening it, she measured it again on the inside and found fully six inches difference in the measurement.

"Just as I thought," she exclaimed. "The trunk has a false bottom."

Examining it carefully, she found that the trunk seemed to be lined with a thick cardboard substance. She pried under this with a steel knife which she had procured from the kitchen and found that it was not attached. Now to get a strong hold on both sides of this fake lining and the whole inside of the trunk ought to come loose.

First Judy had to remove all the dress hangers and drawers as the trunk had been equipped very elaborately. If she had help it would be easy to lift out the interior but she did not intend to let Horace in on the secret. Finally, with the ruler inserted in one side and the knife in the other, she managed to get a grip on each side of the artificial lining. Then she gave a mighty pull.

Just as she had hoped, the whole box-like inside of the trunk gave way and almost sent her sprawling. But she jumped to her feet and, in another instant, was peering into the real bottom of the trunk.

What she saw was a quantity of salt bags tied up with white strings. Of course they contained something more valuable than salt and Judy hastened to open one of them.

She emptied the contents in her lap and found it to be coins and bills, probably loot from some unfortunate grocer's cash register. She opened the next bag and the next bag. All they contained was money and Judy did not take time to count it as she knew it must be turned over to the police immediately.

Then, in the fourth bag, she found jewels. Lorraine's ring was not among them but there were half a dozen more bags to be opened and Judy searched each one eagerly until she came to the next to the last one. She opened it and could not suppress a delighted squeal. There, in her lap, was the object of her quest. Lorraine's ring. Everything else in the bag looked as if it might belong to the Lee family too and, suddenly, Judy had an inspiration. She would keep that one bag and return all the rest. Then, at the party, she would have a most delightful surprise for Lorraine.

Judy concealed the one salt bag in the secret drawer of her dresser, locked it and deposited the key in her pocket book. She had no more than closed it when the door bell rang and she hurried downstairs at the sound of Arthur Far-ringdon-Pett's voice in the hall.

"The ring," she exclaimed, catching sight of the glittering article in his hand. "I might have known it. Either you or Peter Dobbs are always coming along just in time to help me out of all my scrapes."

"I just heard about it this morning," he explained. "I'm not staying at the house, you see. I'm awfully sorry this had to happen. Lois would never have given you the ring if she had known the trouble it would cause."

"It would have been all right if Lorraine's ring hadn't been stolen," Judy answered. "Anyway I thought I could stand it until Lois got well. This getting hard may be good for me. Folks have to learn how to take hard knocks—and I'm learning."

"Good for you. You mean you're shouldering your troubles like a woman instead of like a little girl. But I don't want you to grow up too fast. You're so nice the way you are. You're growing very pretty too. Or is it that new outfit you're wearing?"

"It's the new dress, of course." She was teasing him. She felt like teasing, joking, laughing. It was going to be so wonderful, having the girls trust her again. And now she could plan the party with her whole heart.

"Lorraine's in the car," Arthur said suddenly. "She wants, or to put it more exactly, I want her to talk with you."

Judy followed him as far as the porch but Lorraine had grown tired of waiting and was already walking stiffly over to where they were standing.

"Arthur says that ring is yours," she said, tossing her yellow curls disdainfully. "I think he has made a mistake but it won't mean much anyway after Lois comes back to school."

"Why!" gasped Judy. "What do you mean?"

But Lorraine was gone. Arthur lingered a moment to apologize for her and then followed her back to the car. Judy was not sure whether to be glad or sorry that she had her own friendship ring.

CHAPTER XVIII

INVITATIONS

PLANS for the party progressed as the weeks went by. Lois, a little thinner for her siege with scarlet fever, entered into these plans heartily. Constance, Betty and Marge listened with interest and when Judy told them that Peter Dobbs and Arthur Farringdon-Pett had promised to come, they promised too.

Horace, too, was busy making plans. His plans were more obscure and, therefore, all the more delightful. He handed Judy a little package and she was overjoyed to find that it con-tained printed invitations worded thus:

YOU ARE INVITED TO ATTEND A HALLOWEEN GHOST PARTY

AT THE HOME OF JUDY BOLTON
OCTOBER THIRTY-FIRST

Two Ghosts Will Appear in Person
Please Come Masked

Time: Seven O'clock
Place: Thirteen hundred and sixty-five
Grove Street

ENTERTAINMENT   MUSIC   REFRESHMENTS

All around the edge of the card danced silhouettes of ghosts, goblins and the like and the type was of the finest.

Judy hugged her brother so hard that he gasped for breath. "You darling!" she exclaimed. "You perfect wonder! How did you do it?"

"Easy," he replied, "set the type myself and ran them off on the press after work hours. The Halloween figures are borrowed from an old cut that had been packed away in the shop for years. Nobody else wanted it so Mr. Lee told me I could take it. I suppose his pretty daughter will be getting one of the invitations."

"Yes," replied Judy. "I'm going to invite her. I do hope she comes. It will almost spoil the party if she doesn't."

Judy carried the invitations to school the next day and gave out one to every girl in Lois' crowd. They created enough excitement to suit even the adventure-loving girl from

Roulsville. Lois, especially, seemed delighted with hers and Betty, Marge and Constance Gray all promised to come.

That evening Judy gave Irene her invitation and took three over to the Dobbs family and one to the Chief of Police. He smiled his pleasure and assured Judy that he would be there.

"Be sure and come in costume," she cautioned him. "I don't want anyone to suspect who you are."

The chief smiled.

"Don't worry." His eyes were twinkling roguishly. "There won't anybody suspect. Maybe not even you."

She stayed a few minutes more to answer some of his questions. He had grown genuinely interested in the haunted house mystery and made a great many puzzling inquiries from time to time.

Plans for the party grew more definite as the date approached. The house on Grove Street fairly bristled with mysteries.

Horace spent considerable time by himself and always came down from his room with The Ghost at his heels. His clothing smelt of catnip lately and he was often seen puzzling over the little black notebook. It did no good to question him, however, and Judy liked secrets. Besides, her own plans took most of her time and attention outside of school hours. She shopped for such delightful things as nut and candy cups, paper plates in Halloween colors, decorated crêpe paper, party favors and a Halloween party book containing dozens of helpful suggestions.

Lois went with her on some of these shopping tours and Judy valued her suggestions even more than she valued those in the book. Judy liked to do things systematically and decided to write down all the party activities in the order in which they were to come.

"Don't make it too systematic," cautioned Horace, "and remember this. You've got to allow me at least an hour and no questions asked."

"What hour shall it be?" asked Judy in entire disregard of his last remark. "Want an early hour or a late one?"

"Let me see." Horace deliberated for a moment, studying his black notebook. "Better make it late. Serve your refreshments first and let me have the hour before midnight."

"That leaves the hour after midnight **for** me." Judy was very excited.

"We'll see," promised Horace. "Perhaps I'll answer questions the hour after midnight."

"And perhaps I'll ask a few," Judy teased him as she ran from the room.

Lois had never visited the haunted house. There had always been excuses whenever she had been asked. So, on the day before Halloween, when Judy saw her coming up the steps she could hardly believe her eyes. Most of the decorating had been done the night before, but she was just putting on a few surprise touches here and there. She closed the door quickly and let Lois in through the kitchen.

"We're decorating in there," she explained, indicating the closed door with a wave of her hand. "Don't mind if I keep it secret. It's going to be such a wonderful surprise."

Lois made no reply but simply stood staring at her friend.

"Why, Lois, what is it?" she asked in alarm. "Has something happened?"

"Yes," replied Lois gravely. "Something has. Judy, would you be too disappointed if I didn't come to your party?"

Now it was Judy's turn to stare. "Why, Lois," she implored. "You must come. It wouldn't be much of a party without you."

"It won't be much of a party anyway," declared Lois with a sigh.

"It will be much of a party," Judy retorted. "Why, haven't I planned and shopped and fixed things for weeks? Horace has, too. This very minute he's busy carving jack-o'-lanterns and we're going to have six of them with all different expressions on their faces, all lighted too, and shining. We're going to have a witch to tell fortunes and apples on strings and such refreshments—something I thought up all myself. Why, Lois, the party has to be a success. It simply *has* to be. Look!"

She swung open the door and stood with her back braced against it. Her gray eyes challenged Lois.

"Now, *are* we going to have a party? Doesn't it *look* like a party? Isn't it nice enough for anybody?"

"It is!" cried Lois. "It is a creation and you are marvelous. Oh, Judy, I wish you hadn't done it."

"Why, for Heaven's sake, why?"

"Because—because you are going to be so disappointed. A party isn't a party without a lot of people and nobody will come."

"Who says they won't?" snapped Judy, her temper rising. "Why shouldn't they? Even if they don't like me, they're curious to see what's going to happen. Besides, they promised. At least Constance and Marge and Betty did. Surely such a well-bred crowd as they are would keep their promises."

"They would," replied Lois, "if it weren't for Lorraine. I would too, but now I can't. Oh, I'm so sorry!"

Judy pushed her friend gently into a chair. "Get a breath and then tell me all about it," she said. "What has Lorraine done now and *why* can't you all come to my party?"

Lois opened the dainty lizard skin purse that she carried and withdrew a small white envelope.

"Read this," she said, "and then this," as she displayed a larger envelope directed to herself in Lorraine Lee's handwriting.

CHAPTER XIX

DISAPPOINTMENT

JUDY opened the small envelope first and beheld an invitation very similar to those that she had given out but much more elaborate. It was gilt edged and the figures were in gold instead of black. She read:

A HALLOWEEN PARTY

Witches!   *Goblins!*   *Ghosts!*

Marlin, the great magician will be there in person to summon them for your entertainment.

Rebecca, the gypsy fortune teller, will read your palms and foretell your futures.

MUSIC BY THE VICTOR THEATRE ORCHESTRA

Surprises!   *Excitement!*   *Thrills!*

LORRAINE LEE INVITES YOU

PLEASE COME MASKED AND IN COSTUME

Date: October thirty-first

Time: Seven O'clock

Place: One Sixty Vine Street

"A spite party," said Judy with an indifferent toss of her head. "Well, what of it? I gave out my invitations first, didn't I?"

"I know you did," replied Lois. "But Lorraine is my best friend. We've been pals ever since we were little babies and I can't give her up even if she is unkind to you. I *must* go to her party. Read the other letter and you'll see why."

Judy opened it and read it all the way through without once looking up:

"Dear Lois:

"Your mother tells me that you have decided to go to Judy Bolton's party instead of mine. Lois dear, you have always been the life of my parties. The last one was a perfect flop just because you weren't there. Do you know that for three nights I have walked home from school alone just because you preferred a stranger to your own and your mother's friend? Your mother almost cried when I told her. It has always been her dearest wish that you and I should remain true to our pledge as she and my mother were true to theirs. A friendship that has lasted as long as ours ought to mean more than anything else in the world.

"You may go to Judy's party if you like. But if you do it will mean that you prefer her friendship to mine, that you have given me up *forever.*

"I want to be your best friend as I have always been so please don't force me to be unkind.

"Lovingly,   Lorraine."

"Lovingly," repeated Judy mockingly as she thumped the letter down on the table. "So this is love! Dear little golden-haired Lorraine will never be friendly with you again unless you come to her party, but you can stay away from Judy's party and she will treat you just as sweet as ever. Is *that* what you think, Lois Farringdon-Pett?"

"Oh! Oh! Judy, you are making it hard for me!" And Lois began to cry silently into her handkerchief.

Judy stood there watching her coldly. She had never seen Lois cry before, but found herself strangely unsympathetic. She set her lips tightly together and, without a word, walked out of the room and left Lois there alone, crying.

Horace, on the back porch busy with his last jack-o'-lantern, looked up and saw the determined expression on his sister's face.

"Where's the battle?" he asked, trying to be funny.

"Right here," she replied. "And I'm fighting it. I'm going out after new recruits."

"Now what!" exclaimed Horace. But there was no one to listen to him. Judy was running along the short cut that went behind the houses in the row. He saw her turn in at Sally Belaski's back door. In her hand she carried a pack of white cards that looked like the rest of her party invitations.

Horace did not know that Lois had called and when he saw her dejected figure crumpled in a chair, his eyes grew big. He deposited his last jack-o'-lantern on the floor none too gently and bent over her anxiously.

"I'm afraid my sister hasn't been very polite," he apologized, connecting circumstances as best he could. "She has a quick temper and I hope you will forgive her."

Lois continued to sob.

"Come now," coaxed Horace, "it isn't as bad as all that. Judy always gets over her mad spells."

"She won't get over this one," sobbed Lois. "She'll never get over it. Horace, I'm going now—before she comes back."

"No, no, wait a minute."

But in spite of his protests she ran away and he sat down among the decorations to think things out.

In a little while Judy returned. The party invitations were gone.

"Look here," demanded Horace. "What have you done to Lois?"

"Nothing," she replied coldly, "and Lois has done nothing to me. Our party can get along very well without her."

"Why do you say that?"

"Because," replied Judy, "Lois came to tell me that she is going to Lorraine Lee's party instead of mine. That means that none of her friends will come to my party. I invited Lorraine and had such a wonderful surprise for her but instead of accepting the invitation she plans a party on purpose to spoil mine and Lois likes her well enough to uphold her in all her meanness to me."

"But why did you run away from Lois?"

"Because I couldn't bear to look at her any more." Judy was trembling. "Oh, Horace, I don't know whether I'm going to laugh or scream, but we'll go right on planning the party. The mill girls will come. Lorraine Lee forgot to invite them.''

There was something about the expression on his sister's face that almost frightened Horace. Once he had seen a movie where the captain went down with his ship. The look on the captain's face had been something like that, grim and determined. A girl's face ought not to look like that the day before her party.

''Horace,'' she said suddenly, ''I'm going to quit Girls' High School and go to Industrial High where all the mill girls go. I promised Irene just now. She says people are treated like human beings there. You know Dad says he never gives up a case until his patient is dead. Well, Lois is dead as far as I'm concerned. And Lorraine! It would take something the size of an earthquake to make me like her now.''

During the evening as brother and sister worked together, neither spoke. Judy's swift fingers designed wonders of crêpe paper, cardboard and glue while Horace occupied himself wheeling in autumn leaves and emptying them on the floor until it was completely covered.

He then brought in a tub of water and emptied two dozen apples into it. Each apple had a face grinning from the end of it. The stems of the apples were the noses.

Judy quit her own work and watched him. Next came a maple tree tall enough to touch the ceiling. Horace fastened this in the center of the tub by three wires hooked at the edges. On the top of the tree hung a Halloween lantern in the shape of a goblin's head. Farther down was a nest with paper owls in it. Their eyes shone with light reflected from the lantern. Judy walked over to the tree, stooped and took an apple from the tub and studied its comical face. Suddenly she burst out laughing.

"Watch this!" she cried and before Horace could stop her she had removed Lois' ring from her finger and pushed it through the grinning mouth and into the heart of the apple.

"Stop!"

Horace caught at her arm, but she had thrown the apple back into the tub and it could not be told from the others.

"Some mill girl will be glad to get that ring," she said with a sarcastic smile. "I'll tell them there's a prize in one of the apples. More excitement, you see—and we must have excitement at our party.''

The Chief of Police was surprised the next morning at eight o'clock to see Judy Bolton again standing beside his desk.

''Up all night again?'' she asked.

''Sure. More trouble. Look like you're having some trouble yourself. What's up?''

''My party is spoiled,'' she answered. ''You can stay home that night and get some rest if you like. Here,'' she handed him a white salt bag with the string securely tied. ''I kept these out when I returned the other things because I intended to give them out at the party. Please return them to Mrs. Lee as soon as you can.''

And Judy ran out of the door leaving Chief Kelly sitting there at his desk with a cup of coffee half way to his lips. She heard a crash as she closed the door and hoped he had not broken the cup.

Then she went on to school as usual, recited her lessons exceptionally well, and, at the end of the day, turned in her books.

As she hurried down the stairway she almost collided with Lois. She was wearing the string of blue beads that Judy had given her in exchange for the ruby friendship ring.

"Excuse me," she murmured.

"Certainly," replied Judy coldly. "But why are you wearing my beads?"

"Because—because——"

"You needn't bother to explain," interrupted Judy. "Keep them if you like, but please don't wear them again." She displayed her hand with the five fingers outstretched and Lois saw that the friendship ring was gone.

"Oh!" she exclaimed.

That was all. The two girls separated and one would have never supposed by the expressions on their faces that both were looking forward to parties in the evening.

CHAPTER XX

HALLOWEEN

BY SEVEN o'clock the tables were set, the refreshments prepared and everything in readiness for the party. When the first knock sounded Judy, dressed as a witch in the black evening dress with silver spangles and carrying Blackberry under one arm, hobbled to the door with the aid of a broomstick. A tall peaked hat covered her hair except for a long braid which she had tied with a black tulle ribbon. Blackberry also wore a frill of black tulle and his face peered out as if from a frame.

Two figures in white sheets with round eye-holes cut through, entered and their trailing robes rustled in the carpet of autumn leaves. They were tall figures, but as they refused to speak, Judy could not tell who they were. She bade them be seated in the beautifully decorated room.

Irene had gathered nearly all of her chrysanthemums and these were grouped in among the autumn leaves and some had been saved for table decorations. The dining room and the living room of the haunted house were almost one, but Judy had separated them by a black curtain with Halloween figures cut out and pasted all over it. Yellow light from the six jack-o'-lanterns made the whole room look ghostly. Apples suspended from the ceiling on strings and a fruit dish filled with vegetables and nuts helped preserve the Halloween spirit together with Horace's maple tree with the owl's nest in it. Apples still floated in the tub underneath the tree and, in one of the apples, was Lois' ring. Paper bats clung to the ceiling while paper witches, spiders and cats peered out from unexpected places.

More guests arrived, all masked and in costume. A great many of them were ghosts; several were clowns; others were dressed in gay crêpe paper costumes and one very tall lady had feet that looked surprisingly like a man's. An old man and an old lady dressed in the costumes of fifty years ago, accompanied this awkward tall lady with the large feet.

"Peter!" exclaimed Judy. "I know you. No woman would wear such a massive shoe."

"The idea!" mimicked the tall lady in a high-pitched voice. "This old witch is making personal remarks about my feet. Boo hoo! I can't stand it," and Peter, or whoever it was, began wiping his eyes with the edge of his ruffled petticoat.

This caused more merriment and before she knew what was happening Judy was having such fun that she had almost forgotten that most of her guests were not the ones she had originally invited.

Two girls arrived with two tall escorts. The tall figures were dressed as the Mock Turtle and the Gryphon, characters from Alice in Wonderland. The smaller ones represented the White Rabbit and the Mad Hatter. The costumes were so perfect that Judy knew they must have been made to order.

"Are you Arthur?" she inquired in surprise us she took the hand that the Gryphon offered from underneath one wing.

"What fun!" he exclaimed in imitation of the Gryphon in the story.

Judy puzzled over the Mock Turtle for a considerable time. It was too tall for a girl and it wasn't Peter Dobbs because he had come dressed as a lady.

"Who are you?" she asked at length.

"Once," said the Mock Turtle, "I was a real turtle."

"He's what mock turtle soup is made from," put in the Gryphon.

And Judy laughed, remembering the story.

The next guest to arrive was Alice herself, dressed in the same full skirt and small white apron that she wears in all the pictures.

"Your hair wants cutting," spoke up the Hatter in a girl's voice. Judy guessed that she must have been trained for the part. The queer thing about it all was that Alice looked like Irene. Yes, Judy was almost sure that Alice was Irene. But how could they have known that Irene intended to come dressed as Alice?

"One thing I hadn't thought of," Judy remarked, "is how you are all going to bob for apples with your masks on."

"That's easy," replied a clown, "take our masks off."

"But," cried a ghost, "that will spoil the party."

"Suppose we have a little entertainment first," suggested the Gryphon. "Wasn't that the plan?"

"Quite right," replied Judy. "Just about everybody must be here by now. My! I didn't expect half that many." She had paused and counted twenty-two. "Sit down in the leaves please or, if there are any who object to sitting on the floor——"

A shout interrupted her. "Sit in the leaves! Sit in the leaves! Yeah! Watch out for that owl up there! He looks ugly! Watch out for the bats! Watch out for the cats! Yeah!"

As soon as the noise had subsided, Judy continued. "I can't call on the entertainers because I don't know who you are. First!"

A Halloween fairy dressed in crêpe paper walked up to the doorway and stood beside the curtain. In her arms she carried a violin and, while the jack-o'-lantern lights flickered across her face, she played the Dance of the Ghosts even more exquisitely than she had played it the first time.

"Irene," whispered Judy to Arthur who was sitting beside her, "and I thought that Alice was Irene."

He chuckled softly, but said nothing while Judy studied Alice. She was not Lois. Of that she felt sure. Lois had dark hair and Alice's hair was light, just the shade of Irene's. Lois was taller than the girl who represented Alice, and she was not so slim.

The next act was most amusing. Alice stepped forward and tumbled into a pile of leaves.

"Goodness! What a fall I've had!" she exclaimed just as the White Rabbit turned the corner by the door holding a watch and muttering about the time. In this way they enacted scene after scene from the quaint story until the Gryphon and the Mock Turtle came in for their parts. That was the best of all. The queer figures in costume seated on the floor went off into spasms of laughter at the comical antics of these two. But who was Alice? Why, with all that talking Judy surely ought to recognize her. She had come to the decision that the Mock Turtle was none other than Donald Carter who had shared in that other wonderful party —the spelling bee.

The act grew funnier and funnier. The Mock Turtle (or Donald) had just finished sing-

ing that screamingly funny song of his about
the Beau-ootiful Soo-oop.

"Chorus again!" cried Arthur in exact imi-
tation of the Gryphon in the story.

Donald began, "Soo-oop of the e-e-eve-
ning——"

"The trial's beginning!" shouted a voice
outside the door. Everyone looked up in sur-
prise.

"Just in time," cried a laughing girlish
voice behind an immense playing card. The
Queen of Hearts had arrived and, with her,
the King and the Knave.

They enacted the rest of the play and at
the end of the Queen's conversation with Alice
she shouted loudly, "Off with her head!" and
whisked the mask off the girl who had taken
the part of Alice.

It was Lorraine Lee!

"Off with your masks, everybody!" shouted
a fat figure with a long black moustache and
shell rimmed glasses.

Judy heard him in a daze. People began
taking off their masks. Someone spoke to Judy
and she removed hers. Lorraine was looking
around the room, smiling to people she knew,

but Judy avoided looking at her. She hardly dared hope that Lorraine had come to her party because she really wanted to be friendly.

Lois had been the Queen of Hearts. Her face peered anxiously out of the immense playing card. The King and Knave had been Kay Vincent and Connie Gray and the Mad Hatter and the White Rabbit had been Betty and Marge. Practically all the girls in Lois' crowd were there.

Judy also recognized about a half dozen of Horace's friends, young men from the newspaper office and from the School of Journalism. So many mill girls were there that she did not try to count them.

For some time Peter's grandparents had been busy helping Mrs. Bolton behind the curtains. A familiar whistle sounded (it was Dr. Bolton's) and Horace drew them back. Such an exclamation as went up from the crowd who peered through the doorway! The table groaned with Halloween delicacies, foods in Halloween colors and decorated paper dishes. In the center of the table was a great black pot, steaming with hot tea.

Judy entered, carrying the cat, and began

stirring the tea with a long stick and muttering in a witch-like voice:

"Magic tea, magic tea. What, oh what will
     your future be?
 Magic tea, magic tea. Drink, oh drink me
     and you shall see."

Cups were passed eagerly and filled with
liquid from the black pot.

"Don't stir your tea," called Judy, "or
you'll spoil your fortunes."

"Oh, there's a great tall fellow in mine,"
called Sally Belaski, who had been dressed as
a ghost and had now thrown the sheet back
from her face.

"Who's reading these fortunes?" demanded
Ada, "you or the witch?"

Judy promised to read them all after the
supper was finished and the guests ate faster
in anticipation although some of the foods that
Judy had prepared with her mother's help were
much too pretty to eat.

While some of the guests rushed to have
their fortunes told, others tried biting at the
apples on the strings and in the tub.

Judy had almost forgotten about the ring.

Suddenly she stood up and shouted, "No more ducking for apples in that tub. Has anybody found the prize?"

Nobody answered.

"Maybe somebody swallowed it," suggested Peter Dobbs with a grin.

"I felt something lodge in my windpipe," Arthur said with a loud gulp. "Gee! I guess I did swallow it. Help! Get a surgeon!"

"Arthur!" Judy spoke sternly. "Did anybody really find the prize?"

A chorus of no's was her answer.

"Wait a minute then," she told them, "and I'll put a couple of prizes in these apples hanging on strings. Shut your eyes, everybody, while I do it."

Judy had to think quickly. She had fastened two beauty pins in the shape of half moons into her shawl. She removed them quickly and fastened them again so that no one could be pricked. Then she pressed them into the soft apple pulp.

"Open your mouth and open your eyes!
    Bite the apples and win a prize."

She sang out this hastily-thought-of rhyme and everybody supposed that the party was running smoothly as it was supposed to run. Then she turned to Lois.

"Want to have your fortune told?"

"I'd love it." Lois held out her cup while Judy peered inside it.

"I see a tall dark man," she said.

Lois glanced at Donald Carter who stood across the room talking to Lorraine.

"I see him too," she laughed.

"I see tears and money and friends," Judy went on. "There are a lot of friends but two of them are very fond of you."

"Is that all the fortune?" Lois asked after a pause.

"I guess so."

"Did you read it out of the tea cup?"

"Witches can read it any way they like," Judy replied. "Lois, tell me, what happened —to Lorraine's party?"

"She called it off."

"Why?"

"Really," Lois replied, "I couldn't tell you. It was so sudden that it left us all a little bewildered."

"But you did your 'Alice in Wonderland' act perfectly——"

"We rehearsed our heads off for that," Lois declared. "Hardly stopped for dinner. Lorraine was so determined to make it a success."

Other people crowded around to have their fortunes told—Connie, Betty and Marge and then Lorraine. She held out her cup eagerly but Judy waited, not knowing what to say. The tea leaves were all heaped in one place and, only having studied the art of fortune telling recently, Judy could not understand them.

"It's all a puzzle," she said. "Lorraine, why don't you tell me?"

"There's nothing to say—except thank you —for finding—this." Her voice broke and she held out her hand to show Judy the other ring just like her own.

"Did you have a nice time, Lorraine?" she asked anxiously.

"A simply wonderful time! I never dreamed there'd be so many here. Where did they all come from? And who is that adorable little girl who played the violin?"

"She's one of the silk mill girls. So are

most of the others and the boys are mostly Horace's friends.''

''Quite a mixture,'' laughed Lorraine. ''Here comes the girl now. We'd like to meet her.''

''Horace wants you, Judy,'' whispered Irene when the introductions were completed.

Judy darted swiftly through the crowd.

''Watch the curtain!'' cried some one as Judy stepped up to it and signalled for all of them to be quiet.

Just then the clock began striking—slowly because it needed winding. The hour before midnight had arrived.

CHAPTER XXI

HORACE'S SURPRISE

THE room became as still as a church yard, all eyes eagerly fixed on the swaying curtain and the girl who stood by it. Slowly, over the top of the curtain, shadowy shapes arose and floated out into the room. Their faces were like skeletons, transparent and smooth and their gray robes trailed behind them as they lifted themselves just above the heads of the young people. Some of the girls screamed.

"They won't hurt you," called Judy cheerfully. "They're fakes, like all ghosts. Watch!"

She held up a long hat pin, and flourished it aloft. The point pricked one of the ghosts right in his hollow appearing eye.

Boom! The ghost exploded and fell to the floor while people rushed from right and left to examine what was left of it.

"Why!" exclaimed Donald Carter as he picked up something yellow and sticky from the floor. "It was only a gas balloon with a gray

189

cloth thrown over it and a face painted on with ink.''

"Just so,'' laughed Arthur, "and I wouldn't be at all surprised if Judy herself had painted the face.''

Then the curtain parted and Horace appeared.

"Allow me to present Detective Horace Bolton, Master of Mysteries.''

With a wave of her hand Judy bowed and curtsied, leaving her brother alone before the black curtain.

"Ahem!'' he cleared his throat and began telling in a ministerial tone about all the mysteries connected with number thirteen sixty-five Grove Street since the fatal shooting of its dishonest tenant, Vine Thompson.

"Strange noises were heard,'' he continued solemnly, "and one of the most disturbing of these was a plaintive cry together with a series of scratchings and scrapings as if some imprisoned creature were trying to escape. Listen!''

From behind the curtain came the very noises Horace had described. Whispers of, "that's it,'' and "that's what I heard'' came

of them were caused, no doubt, by the up and down movement of the kitten's tail. Others,'' and here he produced a well-drawn diagram, "were caused by the action of this tree. The branches, when moved by the wind, caused a gentle tap-tapping on the wall which increased at night as the wind grew stronger. I climbed the tree as I suspected the cause of the rappings and, in doing so, split the branch a little more, causing the rappings to change to a scraping which sounded, so my sister said, like some one dragging dead bodies across a bare floor. She persuaded me to climb the tree again and, while she and some of our neighbors watched, I removed several thousand dollars worth of stolen jewelry from the hollow break in the branch. We immediately returned the valuables to the police department and afterwards received a five-hundred-dollar reward which we divided between us. The scraping sound I stopped by roping the two branches of the tree so tightly together that they could not possibly touch the sides of this house.''

"But the voice?" cried Sally Belaski who could stand the suspense no longer. "How do you explain Vine Thompson's voice?"

"How many heard it?" inquired Horace. At least a dozen hands went up into the air.

"It was the voice that scairt people away," declared Ada O'Malley. "They could of stood the rest, but that spooky voice is what got 'em."

Horace grinned. "I'm coming to that if you'll be patient. First I want to explain the lights. You say they flashed on and off at all hours of the night. That may be. Poker players are not afraid of ghosts once they have found a quiet spot where they can gamble without being molested. At any rate, gamblers were there. I found a few things on the floor when we first moved in which will prove that to your satisfaction."

He displayed a few poker chips, some well-fingered playing cards and a quantity of discarded cigar and cigarette butts.

"The idea of a respectable reporter carrying around such things as that," teased Arthur good-naturedly.

"Before I'm through," retorted Horace, "you will see that I have carried around much worse things than that. I am about to explain the mystery of the voice. Are there any questions before I begin?"

"Let's have the questions afterwards," shouted Donald Carter, one of those who had heard the voice.

"Very well," began Horace, but the kitchen clock, striking the long hour of midnight, interrupted him.

Everybody waited, breathless. The curtain was rolled slowly back revealing what appeared at first glance to be an empty bird cage. Horace held it up and turned it slowly around, letting a shaft of yellow light shine from one of the jack-o'-lantern's directly into it. The cage was not empty. Inside lay the same dead thing that Judy had seen, and smelled, up in the attic. Her brother reached in through the open door of the cage and removed this gruesome object. As he did so, one of its bony legs dropped off and rattled to the floor. Some of the girls screamed.

"It won't hurt you," said Horace calmly. "It has been dead a long time. In fact, I think it has been dead about two months." He studied his black book for a moment. "Yes, it must have been dead for at least two months. It has been all of that since you heard the voice, has it not. Donald?"

Donald Carter nodded. "That's right, Horace. I think the voice has been silent since that time."

Peter Dobbs sat looking confused and bewildered, while Horace continued to expound his theories concerning the dead thing that he held in his hands.

"Observe its beak, if you please—and its claws." He stooped to pick up the one that had fallen among the leaves on the floor. "What kind of a bird would you say this was?"

"A magpie, by gum," exclaimed Mr. Dobbs from his seat in the corner. "By golly, where did that come from?"

"From our attic," explained Horace, "where all the other mysteries were hidden. The question that now arises is this: Why were they hidden there?"

Again Horace consulted his notebook. "Old Vine Thompson's house was searched and emptied of all its furnishings on July tenth of this year. Let us assume that the old lady tried to hide some of her valuables. It seems the things she cared most for were the stolen jewels which she, or some member of her gang, concealed in the hollow tree; her clothes, her magpie and her cat; also her gun which Peter Dobbs returned to the police station.

"As many of you know, our attic is a hard place to get at. You enter it through a small hole in the ceiling of my sister's bedroom and it is all that a fat person could do to squeeze in there. Fortunately, Vine Thompson was not fat. This is what must have happened from the information that I have been able to gather. Some time before July tenth, possibly the day before, she gathered these valuables together and stored them in her attic. Not knowing exactly what her fate would be at the hands of the police she made ample provision for her pets by leaving a large supply of food and water for both the cat and the magpie. The latter lived a little less than a month but in that time he frightened three families away by his weird imitation of his mistress' voice. He was dead when we moved in here and that is why neither myself nor any member of my family have heard the voice——"

"Hold on there!" shouted Peter Dobbs. "We heard the voice two weeks ago—your sister, Irene Lang and myself. I'd just like to know how your dead magpie explains that!"

CHAPTER XXII

JUDY'S SOLUTION

HORACE was silent. They had him cornered at last.

"You said you'd answer questions," Judy spoke up, "and I said I'd ask them. Are you ready?"

Horace nodded.

"Dead magpies don't talk, do they?" asked Judy. "Well then, your dead bird wasn't the only cause of the voice. Furthermore, Vine Thompson never put those things in the attic because she was killed before they were put there. The Chief of Police says that the attic was searched and left empty except for a few old papers that weren't worth carting away.

"My theory is that some robber who wanted to conceal stolen goods put the cat and the bird up there on purpose to scare people. From what Chief Kelly says that would be the sort of trick that Vine Thompson's youngest son would be apt to play. He's supposed to be so clever. Are you ready for more questions?"

Horace nodded again. He seemed incapable of speech.

"Well, cats don't eat lettuce, do they?"

"No."

"And cats don't eat cucumbers, do they?"

"No, of course not. What are you driving at?" Horace asked impatiently.

"Well, that food we found couldn't have been put up there to feed cats. Some one must have been hiding in the house. And when we came they must have escaped through the attic window, split the branch of the tree so that they could scramble down and make a get-away."

"By golly!" exclaimed Mr. Dobbs. "If that isn't the cleanest piece of detective work I ever saw in all my life!"

"Somebody's been going in and out of the attic ever since," Judy went on. "Remember, Horace, how you found the rope had been taken off your tree. Well, it was that same afternoon that we heard the voice. Somebody climbed up your tree and in through the attic window and tried to scare us. They wanted to get us out of the house so that they could haul away the trunk.''

"For Heaven's sakes! Why?" exclaimed her brother. "There was nothing but some old clothes in the trunk."

"Are you sure?"

"No," Horace replied. "I've given up being sure of things."

"Peter," Judy directed. "You and Horace go upstairs, like good boys, and bring down the trunk. It isn't very heavy now it's empty."

Everybody sat entranced. This was a party such as they had never expected to attend. Anything might happen.

Presently Peter and Horace returned. But the trunk was not between them. The blank expressions on their faces gave eloquent proof that something was wrong.

"Where? Why? What?" stammered Judy.

"The trunk is gone." It was Peter who gave out this startling information.

"It couldn't be," Judy exclaimed. "We would have heard—" Then she remembered the noise they had been making. "No, maybe we wouldn't——"

She stopped short. A thunderous **rap** sounded at the door.

Dr. Bolton, who seemed to have kept his head through all the excitement, swung the door **wide** open and there stood the Chief of Police.

Judy rushed forward to greet him.

"But you're so late—" she began.

"Well, seeing you invited me, I thought I might bring along a couple of guests."

He pushed into the light two figures, one tall and thin; the other short and stumpy. Their wrists were securely handcuffed together.

"Explaining ghosts, weren't you?" he went on with a chuckle. "Well, here's the liveliest looking pair of ghosts I ever saw. I just now caught them climbing down the lattice with an empty trunk between them. Thought there were jewels in it, eh?"

He turned to the two figures who answered with sullen grunts. They had come forward into the room and Judy recognized them both. Just as she suspected, the short one was Irene's troublesome boarder. The other she knew only from the faded photograph that she had found in the trunk. He was Vine Thompson's elusive son. The mill girls were staring at him in open-mouthed amazement, and Judy remembered that he was supposed to have been carried off to the land of spirits. As soon as he spoke she recognized the "voice."

"Well," he asked the chief, "seeing you're so hospitable, can't we sit down and enjoy the party?"

"Your party's in a cell in the county jail," Chief Kelly replied gruffly. "You're clever, but not so clever as you think you are. That house-breaking stunt of yours is an old one. A good many burglars try sneaking into houses when a party's going on. Humph!" He gave Judy a sidelong glance, "but not this kind of a party. I'll be back," he called from the door, "as soon as these ghosts are locked up."

"How did he happen to catch them?" Horace asked in surprise after the chief had closed the door.

"I invited him to the party," Judy replied. "And just to make sure nobody recognized him, he stayed outside. He told me he might be needed. Now shall I continue with my act?"

A howl of assent went up from the excited crowd.

"You see," she continued, smiling, "it's just

as I said, those men were trying to get at the trunk, but they were a little too late. I opened it myself with a nail file and," she paused. "May I take the trunk?"

The chief had left it near the doorway and Arthur shoved it to the center of the room.

"Will somebody lend me a ruler?" Judy asked.

Her father stepped forward with a folding yardstick and she began measuring the trunk, first the outside; then the inside.

"You see the difference? Chief Kelly told me to use my head and this is the result. I discovered that the trunk had a false bottom and underneath were the things that the men who climbed the tree were trying to get hold of. They couldn't carry the trunk through the attic window and down the tree and so they had to wait until we were out of the way. If it hadn't been for Chief Kelly outside they would have carried it away over the porch roof and down the lattice. They must have shoved it out through my bedroom window."

"Ugh!" Irene shivered. "And to think they were trying to get in your room all this time."

"Yes. Remember, Horace, the night I woke

up and screamed. That was the same night they pulled off that robbery at the other end of town."

"The one I reported!" he exclaimed. "Sure. Come to think of it, these men do fit the description that woman gave us."

"And I shouldn't be surprised," Judy continued, "if they are the last of Vine Thompson's gang."

"But you didn't tell us what was in the trunk!" exclaimed one of the mill girls.

"More stolen jewelry," Judy replied, and then sat down.

There was an awkward moment of silence. There seemed to be a general feeling that Judy had not revealed all she knew.

Then Irene spoke up. "The love letters?" she questioned. "What about them?"

"What love letters?" cried several voices.

"Oh, just a pack of old letters I found in the attic. They're too sad to read at a party and it is so late."

"Who wrote them? Why were they sad? Oh, I'd love to hear them." These and many other exclamations greeted this statement.

"Aw, it'll queer the whole party if we don't

hear the love letters," sighed Sally Belaski.
"Go ahead, read 'em."

Judy was already turning the yellowed sheets
of paper and when she found the first letter she
proceeded to read.

At the same moment the Chief of Police, who
had returned sooner than they expected, seated
himself quietly in the corner beside Dr. Bolton.

CHAPTER XXIII

THE DOBBS' FAMILY SECRET

"DEAREST Jimmie Boy:" she began, and Mrs. Dobbs' face went pale. Judy's mother who sat beside her noticed it at once and hurried to get the spirits of ammonia. She fancied that Mrs. Dobbs, like herself, might be subject to dizzy spells.

Judy read all the way through the first letter, not noticing, but just as she was about to read Grace's name, Mr. Dobbs leaned forward in his chair and shouted "Stop!"

Everybody stared as, red faced and trembling he went on, "I say, isn't there anything better for you young folks to do than sneak off and pry into somebody's love letters? Here, let me have the letters. They're nobody else's business."

This was a most startling thing to happen at a party. Mrs. Dobbs had turned as white as any of the sheeted ghosts and was smelling ammonia as if her life depended on it.

"Sounds as if the old gentleman knew something about it," one of the mill girls whispered.

"Sure does," agreed another and Judy heard. Mr. Dobbs lurched forward to grab the letters but she thrust them behind her before he had the chance.

"Just what *is* your claim to these letters, Mr. Dobbs?" she demanded.

The old man stared at her without answering.

"How will it be if I give the letters to Peter and let him figure things out for himself?" Judy went on. "He might be interested in knowing a little more about his mother."

"My mother! Good grief, was I 'Petey boy'? Tell me, granddad. You must tell me. Was Grace your little girl?"

Tears welled to the old man's eyes and he stumbled back to his chair.

"You tell him, grandma," he mumbled. "I haven't got the strength."

Mrs. Dobbs rose to her feet. She was no longer pale but smiled with pride as she drew Peter to her.

"It *is* true, dear grandson," she said. "Grace Dobbs was your mother. I've been wanting to tell you for years and years but your grandfather wouldn't let me.''

"And Vine Thompson's son is my father,'' sighed Peter.

All the boyish animation had gone out of his face.

"Oh, Peter," cried Judy, "do forgive me. It was just this beastly passion I have for solving things. It never occurred to me how you would take it. To think that I've gone ahead and helped corner a robber and then been stupid enough to try and prove that you were related to him.''

"Don't let that worry either of you," said Chief Kelly, smiling at Judy and Peter. "There's none of old Vine's blood in you, Peter. Your father must have been James, the oldest of the three sons.''

"That's right," Peter remembered. "His name was James.''

"Well," chuckled the chief. "James Thompson was old Vine's stepson and the best one of the lot.''

"Then he wasn't a crook?''

"Not that I know of," replied the Chief of Police. "He got killed in an automobile accident when he was only about twenty-two."

"So that's why he didn't answer my mother's letters!" exclaimed Peter with some relief. "And those letters from him all mentioned checks or sums of money and it looks as if old Vine had kept the money and never mailed the letters. What a bad woman old Vine must have been!"

"Golly!" exclaimed Mr. Dobbs. "And I never knew but what he was her own son. That's why we were so set against Grace marrying him."

Mrs. Dobbs turned to Judy with gratitude in her face.

"My dear child," she murmured. "You have added ten years to my life. What could be more beautiful than for a son to keep the memory of his mother in her old love letters. Poor little Grace! What a wrong we have done her in not telling Peter before."

All at once Mr. Dobbs began to chuckle softly to himself. Judy stared at him, hoping that he had not suddenly lost his mind.

"By crackey," he exclaimed, thumping his hand down on her shoulder. "Judy's got me beat every time. First 'twas the spelling bee and now it's the boy. If I'd had common horse sense I'd have told him years ago. Come on, Peter, aren't you going home with your old grandparents?''

"Gee, Judy," Peter said gratefully as he wrung her hand. "You're the cleverest girl in the continent. There isn't another kid in America that could have figured things out the way you did."

The cheer that went up from the rest of the party showed that they all heartily agreed with Peter.

Then Lois turned to Judy and whispered. "Before we go home, won't you please put my ring back on your finger? You have forgiven me, haven't you?"

"A hundred times over," she replied. "I'm beginning to understand how you feel about Lorraine too and I hope we can all be friends."

"But the ring?"

"Lois dear," Judy answered in a penitent voice. "I have a confession to make. When I felt so angry with you I put the ring inside one of those apples over in the tub. Remember, I told them there was a prize in one of the apples?"

"Oh!" Disappointment and remorse sounded in Lois' voice.

"But I'll get it in a minute," called Judy as she darted in the kitchen after a paring knife. "You heard me call out for them to stop biting the apples. Nobody got the prize so it must still be in one of these apples. Oh, dear! It's not in this one."

She had dissected an apple until it was fit only for apple sauce but no ring had turned up.

"Get some more knives and we'll help," offered Lorraine who had also stayed longer than the others waiting for Lois. The apples were soon cut into thin slices. Still no ring!

"Somebody got it and didn't tell," moaned Judy. "Oh, I suppose I deserve it. It was an awful thing to do. Perhaps I'll get over my mean temper some time."

At this moment Horace and Arthur entered the room. They had been exploring the house and talking over the many discoveries of the last few weeks.

"This finishes the investigation," Horace declared solemnly. "Our house is no longer a haunted house. In fact, there are no more mysteries in it."

As he made that statement, Horace had no idea that within a very short time his sister would be endeavoring to solve the most baffling mystery that had ever confronted her and that the house would be haunted, not with ghosts but with music in "The Invisible Chimes."

Now Arthur observed the girls. "What's this?" he asked. "Making apple sauce at two o'clock in the morning. The very idea!"

Judy looked up with a tragic expression in her gray eyes. "We're not making apple sauce. We're looking for my ring."

Arthur smiled broadly. "Perhaps somebody got it and didn't tell."

"That's what I think," declared Lorraine.

Then Arthur held up the ring triumphantly. "You're right," he cried. "That somebody was myself. I suspected it was never meant to be a prize. Hold out your finger, Judy."

"No," protested Lois childishly. "I want to put it on her finger. It's my pledge of friendship."

"Suppose we all do it," suggested Arthur. "Then Judy will have three friends pledged to everlasting loyalty."

Laughing, Judy held out her hand while first

Arthur, then Lorraine and then Lois pushed the ring a little farther on her finger.

Afterwards Lorraine pressed an envelope into her hand and Judy stared at it for fully a minute. She had forgotten that Mrs. Lee had offered a reward for the recovery of the stolen jewels. Perhaps that was because the reward of Lorraine's friendship was so much more important.

Dr. Bolton came into the room just as the last guest departed to remind Judy that it would soon be daylight. "Even detectives have to sleep," he said, "but, Judy girl, don't think for a minute that your Dad doesn't appreciate what you have done for Peter and Lorraine and all of us."

THE END